DK ESSENTIAL INTERNET GUIDE

DK ESSENTIAL INTERNET GUIDE

A Dorling Kindersley Book

Dorling Kindersley
LONDON, NEW YORK, SYDNEY, DELHI,
PARIS, MUNICH, and JOHANNESBURG

Produced for Dorling Kindersley Limited by
Design Revolution, Queens Park Villa,
30 West Drive, Brighton, East Sussex BN2 2GE

EDITORIAL DIRECTOR Ian Whitelaw
SENIOR DESIGNER Andy Ashdown
PROJECT EDITOR John Watson
DESIGNERS Andrew Easton and Paul Bowler

SENIOR EDITOR Mary Lindsay
SENIOR MANAGING ART EDITOR Nigel Duffield
DTP DESIGNER Jason Little
PRODUCTION CONTROLLER Wendy Penn
US EDITOR Gary Werner

First American Edition, 2000

01 02 03 04 05 10 9 8 7 6 5 4 3 2

Published in the United States by Dorling Kindersley Publishing, Inc.
95 Madison Avenue, New York, New York, 10016

Color reproduced by First Impressions, London
Printed in Spain by Gráficas Estella

For our complete
catalog visit
www.dk.com

004.678
D626
c.1

ABOUT THIS BOOK

The *Essential Internet Guide* is an easy-to-follow guide to using your PC to explore the internet, with explanations of everything from modems and browsers to search engines and metatags.

THIS BOOK WILL HELP YOU TO GET THE most out of the internet. In a series of five sections, the *Essential Internet Guide* shows you how to get onto the internet, how to visit websites, how to search for the information, files, and images that you want, how to use email to communicate with people all around the world, and how to build your own website.

Each section is divided into chapters that deal with specific topics, and within each chapter you will find subsections that cover self-contained procedures. Each of these procedures builds on the knowledge that you will have accumulated by working through the previous chapters.

The chapters and subsections use a step-by-step approach, and almost every step is

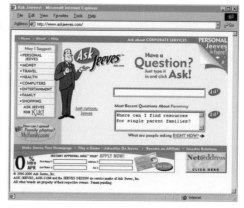

accompanied by an illustration showing how your screen should look.

The book contains several other features that make it easier to absorb the quantity of information that is provided. Cross-references are shown within the text as left- or right-hand page icons: ◁ and ▷. The page number within the icon and the reference are shown at the foot of the page.

As well as the step-by-step sections, there are boxes that explain the meaning of unfamiliar terms and abbreviations, and give additional information to take your knowledge beyond that provided on the rest of the page. Finally, at the back, you will find a glossary explaining new terms, and a comprehensive index.

For further information on computer software and digital technology, see the wide range of titles available in the *DK Essential Computers* series.

CONTENTS

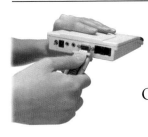

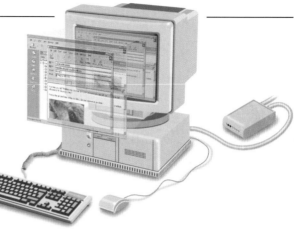

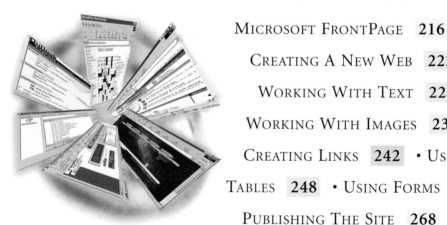

GETTING
CONNECTED

GETTING CONNECTED is an easy-to-follow guide to connecting your PC to the internet, and an introduction to all that the net has to offer, including the world wide web and email. This section will help you get connected using Windows 98, which contains all the software you need to connect you to the internet and to find your virtual feet there. It will help you to choose the right modem and Internet Service Provider for your needs, and make your first connection to the net. It will also show you how to start looking around the web, read newsgroups, send email, and chat online with other users. You will soon be able to search for information, save web pages that are of particular interest to you, download software to your own computer, and access online games.

WHAT IS THE INTERNET?

The internet is a network of millions of computers, offering information, communication, and a wealth of online activities. This chapter describes what it is and how it works.

WHAT CAN YOU DO ON THE INTERNET?

As you read this sentence, millions of people are using the internet. They may be browsing documents on the World Wide Web, exchanging messages by email, chatting "live" in 3D virtual worlds, downloading the latest software, or playing 3D interactive games against players from all over the world.

Your ISP •
The Internet Service Provider acts as the gateway through which the data passes to and from your computer

Your computer
You access the internet from your PC connected by a modem to an ISP •

• Telephone line

Modem
A modem turns digital data into an analog signal to send over the telephone lines to your ISP, and converts received signals into a digital form

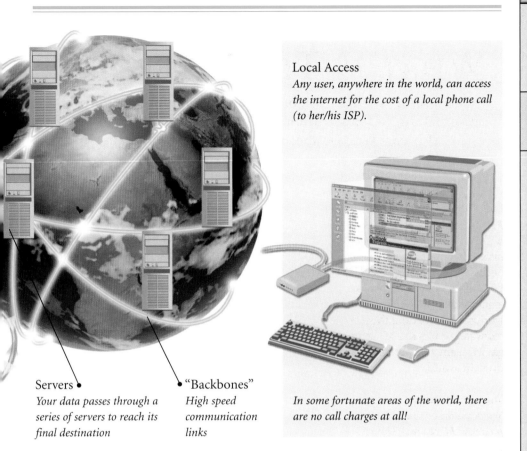

Local Access
Any user, anywhere in the world, can access the internet for the cost of a local phone call (to her/his ISP).

Servers •
Your data passes through a series of servers to reach its final destination

• "Backbones"
High speed communication links

In some fortunate areas of the world, there are no call charges at all!

HOW DOES IT WORK?

The internet, in physical terms, is a vast global network made up from many thousands of computer networks and individual computers. The internet "works" because these computers and computer networks can all speak the same language, called TCP/IP (which stands for Transmission Control Protocol/Internet Protocol).

For most people, the internet is the same thing as the World Wide Web and all the web addresses that appear everywhere these days – on product packaging, at the end of TV shows, and on junk mail. But there is more to the internet than the web.

There are vast networks of computers devoted to newsgroups, bulletin boards and discussion groups ⌐, and thousands of servers across the world are devoted to online "chat" areas ⌐.

But the web is the part of the internet that has seen such a rapid explosion in popularity and ease-of-use.

52 Newsgroups

58 Chat Rooms

WHAT'S ON THE INTERNET?

The internet offers information on just about every topic you care to think of. Whether your interests include current affairs, astrophysics, golf, or Antarctic flora and fauna, there is almost certain to be a website devoted to that topic somewhere.

The net has always been the home of academic information, but it has increasingly become an information base for public sector bodies, government departments, individuals, and, most recently, commercial organizations.

Online games
Pit your wits against opponents all round the world with online games

Email
Communicate with people around the globe for just the price of a local call

Shopping
Online shopping is becoming very big business on the web

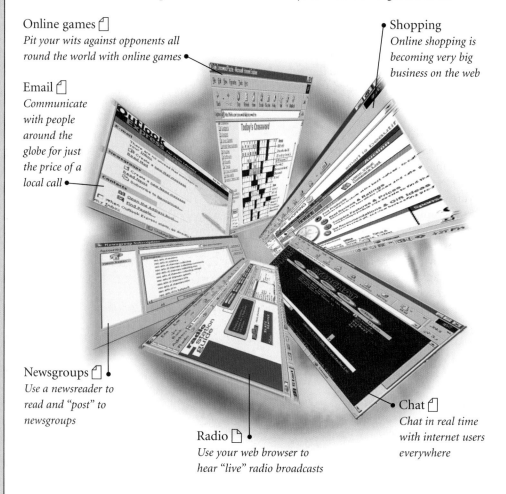

Newsgroups
Use a newsreader to read and "post" to newsgroups

Radio
Use your web browser to hear "live" radio broadcasts

Chat
Chat in real time with internet users everywhere

48 **Online gaming**

56 **Using Email**

52 **Newsgroups**

58 **Chat Rooms**

47 **Radio**

REQUIREMENTS

If you have Windows 98 installed on your computer, you will already have the software required to connect to the internet. But you also need a modem and an account with an Internet Service Provider to make a connection.

MODEM

If you don't have a modem , you will need to buy and install one. If your PC is running Windows 98, it can handle what the internet has to offer, although as video, audio, and real-time broadcasts become more widespread, you'll inevitably begin to think about the need to upgrade your modem or computer hardware.

Your modem connects you to an ISP's systems room

SERVICE PROVIDER

With a PC and modem you need one more element to get connected. That's where your Internet Service Provider (ISP) comes in ⌐. There are numerous ISPs, and many offer free connection and unlimited time online. Some ISPs are obviously more reliable than others, so many users prefer to pay for a proven service.

HARDWARE REQUIREMENTS

In order to connect to the internet you will need: a computer, a modem and connecting cable, and an active telephone line.

16 Modems

23 Choosing a Service Provider

SOFTWARE AND HARDWARE

Microsoft® Internet Explorer is one of the most popular web-browsing programs and offers all the facilities that you need to browse the web and become part of the online community.

WHAT CAN EXPLORER DO?

Internet Explorer comes as a standard part of Windows 98 software and is usually pre-installed on most new computers. Internet Explorer is more than just a web-browsing program: it is a suite of programs enabling most internet-related activities, from browsing the web and composing and sending email, to taking the plunge and publishing your own web pages. Outlook Express is the name of the email program and newsreader that comes with Internet Explorer, and FrontPage® is Microsoft's web-publishing program. Both these programs are covered in their own sections in this book, but a brief description of all three programs will help to give you an idea of what each of them can do and how they are interrelated.

WHAT IS EXPLORER?

Internet Explorer is the web-browsing program that enables you to connect to websites and view them ⬐, surf the web using hypertext links, and download files and programs from the internet to your own computer ⬐. By default, its email features operate through Outlook Express.

⬐ 36 **Onto The Web**

⬐ 50 **Downloading From the Internet**

OUTLOOK EXPRESS

Outlook Express 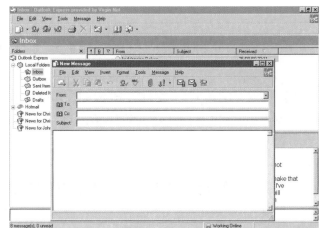 is an email program that you can use to send and receive email, manage your own online address book, and exchange files and information with others over the internet. It also contains a fully featured newsreader for reading and posting messages to internet newsgroups.

FRONTPAGE

Eventually, the time may come when you want to create your own web pages. FrontPage helps you to do just that. It provides a web-page editor that enables you to build web pages with only a minimal understanding of HyperText Markup Language (HTML), the language in which web pages are constructed.

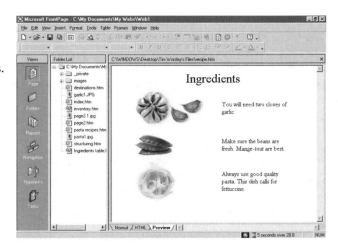

INSTALLING OTHER COMPONENTS

If Outlook Express or FrontPage are not on your computer, you can install them from your Windows or Internet Explorer CD-ROM. If you cannot locate your disks, another option open to you is to download a new version of Internet Explorer from the Microsoft website and reinstall the entire program on your computer, making sure that you elect to install these additional programs during the installation process. Click the **Microsoft** button on the **Links** bar to go to Microsoft's website.

176 Outlook Express

174 Email

214 Building A Website

MODEMS

Without a modem in your computer or connected externally, your connection to the internet remains purely theoretical! The next few pages are devoted to one of the most commonly used types of modem: the 56K V90-compliant external modem. This is capable of receiving data at 56,000 bits per second.

WHAT IS A MODEM?

A modem is a piece of equipment that connects your PC to the internet via the telephone lines. In very simple terms, a modem converts digital (binary) signals from your computer into analog (sound) signals that can be sent along telephone lines. At the same time, it converts incoming analog signals into binary signals (basically, strings of 1s and 0s) that your computer can understand.

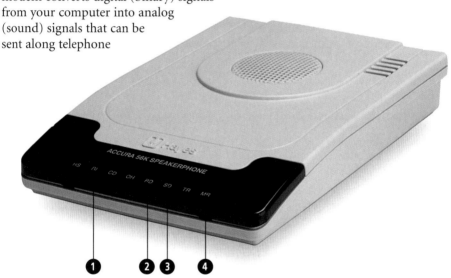

MODEM FRONT PANEL

1 HS – High Speed
This light illuminates if the modem is operating at speeds in excess of 4,800bps.

2 RD – Receiving Data
This light indicates whether or not your modem is "idle."

3 SD – Sending Data
This light is active when you are sending data.

4 MR – Modem Ready
This light shows that the modem is switched on and ready for use.

WHAT IS ISDN?

Integrated Service Digital Network lines can send digital rather than analog information over existing telephone lines at very high speeds, achieving rates of between 64,000 bps and 300,000 bps. It is virtually error-free and can be used to transmit voice. To use ISDN, however, you will need to use special hardware, software, and a different telephone connection and ISP account than those featured in this book. Some service providers charge higher rates for ISDN connections but many do not.

AN EXTERNAL MODEM

The modem in these photographs is a Hayes Accura 56K Speakerphone. This is a good example of an external modem as it has many features, including answering machine, fax, and speakerphone. Obviously there are many other modems available, and some of these may have differing features. The annotation on this example therefore only explains the major features.

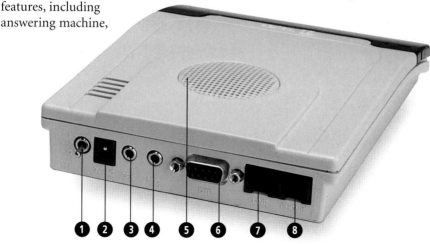

MODEM BACK PANEL

❶ On/Off Switch

❷ Connector
Power supply.

❸ Speaker Connection

❹ Microphone Connection

❺ Speaker

❻ Serial Port (DTE Interface)
For connecting your computer to the modem.

❼ Line
Plug one end of your telephone cable in here.

❽ Phone
To use a telephone on the same line as the modem.

SOFTWARE FOR EXTERNAL MODEMS

When you buy an external modem, it will usually come with its own software on a CD or floppy disk set. Follow the instructions in the manual carefully and you should have few problems installing the software on your computer. The example below shows the software that comes with the Hayes Accura 56K Speakerphone, as shown on the previous pages. Your software may look different, but this screen shows features common to similar modems.

Telephone facility
Shows last call and has its own telephone book, where you can enter your favorite numbers. You can "dial" numbers straight from your keyboard

Answering machine/Voicemail
Enables easy set-up of voicemail and answering machine messages. Play, forward, and rewind messages from this panel

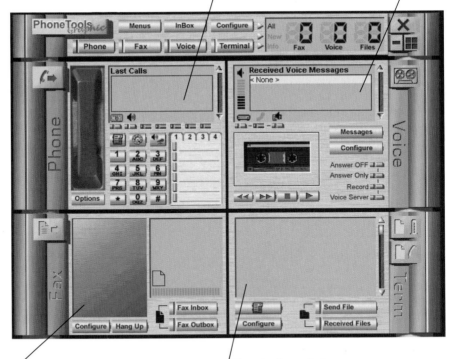

Fax
From this panel you can set up the software to fax a document from any Windows application

Terminal emulation
Connect to various online services to retrieve information, upload and download files, etc.

CHOOSING A MODEM

The most important thing to consider when buying a modem is speed. You want the fastest modem you can afford. The fastest modem currently available is a 56K modem. This means that it is capable of receiving data at 56 Kilobytes per second (although it is only capable of sending data at a maximum of 33.6 Kbps).

WHAT NEXT?

After finding the fastest, most reliable, most economical modem, you need to choose between an internal and external model. If your PC came with an internal modem installed, this won't really concern you – yet. But if modems continue to increase in speed (and drop in price) you may soon find that you want to replace your existing modem.

External modems are very easy to install. There are two stages to installation: first, physical installation (which basically involves plugging things in), and secondly software configuration (which is usually "automatic" with Windows 98).

Installing or replacing an internal modem isn't too difficult either, but if you don't feel happy about taking off the case of your computer and installing a card on the PC's motherboard (remembering to wear an anti-static wrist strap) then you have two choices: either get your hardware dealer to install it for you, or buy an external modem.

One of the major advantages of an external modem is that the lights on the casing indicate the status of your connection, making it easier to know when to restart your internet connection, simply by switching off your modem. With an internal modem, if there is a problem with your internet connection, you may need to restart your computer.

Internal modem
Installing a card on the mother-board of a PC can seem an intimidating task, but is actually fairly straightforward.

INSTALLING AN EXTERNAL MODEM

Connecting an external modem is usually a straightforward task. It is important to read the manufacturer's instructions in case there are any special requirements, but most installations follow the procedure described here.

1 PREPARING TO INSTALL
- Switch off your PC and unplug from the main power supply.

2 CONNECTING POWER SUPPLY
- Connect your modem to the power supply using the cable and/or power adapter provided.

3 CONNECTING SERIAL CABLE
- Attach one end of the serial cable to the modem, and the other end to a vacant serial cable on your PC. This will usually be the COM 1 port, but if your mouse is already installed there, use the COM 2 port.

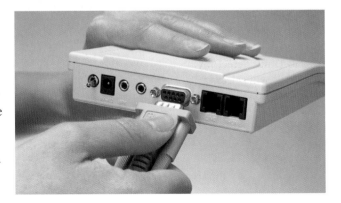

4 TELEPHONE LINE

● Connect the modem's telephone cable between the socket on the modem and the telephone socket. Switch on the modem. One or more of the indicator lights will light up. Switch on the PC and restart it.

CONFIGURING YOUR MODEM

If you are installing a modem that is not accompanied with installation software, Windows 98 will usually detect its make and model automatically. It will then attempt to install all the drivers necessary to make your modem perform effectively. You may find, however, that Windows 98 needs help to locate the appropriate software for your modem. This is usually solved simply by following these steps:

1 MODEMS ICON

● Double-click the **Modems** icon; the **Install New Modem** dialog box will appear.

2 SELECTING MODEM

● Click on the check box next to **Don't detect my modem; I will select it from a list** to tick it, and then click **Next>**.

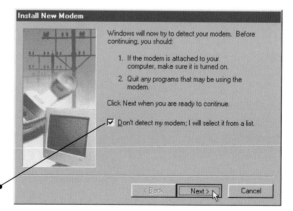

Checkbox ●

3 MANUFACTURER AND MODEL

• Click the appropriate entry under **Manufacturers** and **Models**, then click **Next**. (If the manufacturer has supplied a disk, click **Have Disk…**, navigate to the appropriate location for the CD-ROM or floppy disk, and follow the on-screen instructions.)

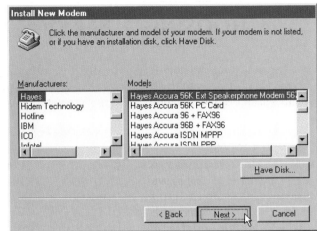

4 SELECTING A PORT

• Click **Communications Port (COM 1)** and then click **Next**. (This may be COM 2 if a mouse is already installed on COM 1.)

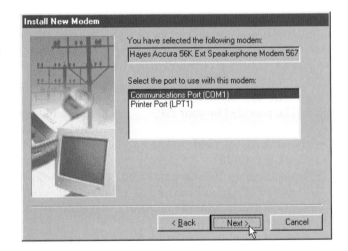

5 COMPLETING THE PROCESS

• Provide the necessary information in the location information dialog box and click **Finish**. Your modem is now ready to use.

CHOOSING A SERVICE PROVIDER

An Internet Service Provider (ISP) provides your gateway to the internet – usually via an ordinary telephone line.

Your ISP will provide you with a local telephone number (a point of presence), which gives you access to its servers.

DIAL-UP ACCESS

This access to servers is known as "dial-up access." If an ISP doesn't provide you with a dial-up connection charged at local rates (or free), you're not interested! An ISP provides you with a number of internet services: access to the web ⌐, a unique email address (perhaps several) ⌐, and access to thousands of newsgroups ⌐. Most ISPs also give you space on their servers to post your own web pages. You may be provided with free software to do all or some of these things.

These are now standard services and should be provided by your ISP.

HOW DO I CHOOSE THE RIGHT ONE?

Choosing the right ISP was much simpler a few years back. If you lived outside urban areas, it was usually a case of finding one that offered internet access at local call

THE INTERNET-READY PC

Most new PCs are advertised as "internet-ready." This means that they contain an internal modem, and a ready-to-go internet account, in which case your ISP is already chosen for you.

rates – if you were lucky! Nowadays, service providers (many offering national coverage) are falling over each other to win your custom, so it's never been a better time to get connected.

The old established ISPs have improved, and newer start-ups are offering excellent deals. A wave of "free" ISPs has also arrived – some are freer than others ⌐.

Meanwhile, the big online service providers (AOL, Prodigy, CompuServe and MSN) have changed their approach to meet the challenge.

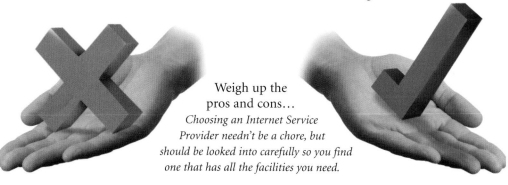

Weigh up the
pros and cons…
Choosing an Internet Service
Provider needn't be a chore, but
should be looked into carefully so you find
one that has all the facilities you need.

| 36 | Onto The Web | 31 | Setting Up an Email Account | 52 | Newsgroups | 25 | Questions to ask an ISP |

HOW DOES AN ISP WORK?

Although it seems you are connected directly to the internet when you are browsing through web pages, all the data you send and receive is actually passing down a lot of cable and through many other computers (servers) before it reaches your screen. All this technical stuff is handled in the background by your ISP.

WHEN YOU ARE CONNECTED

Each time you dial up to the internet, your data is first received and processed by your ISP. If you are requesting data from, or sending data to, the internet, your ISP routes the information via one of its very fast connections to the internet.

If you are requesting or sending email, data is sent to the ISP's mail servers – one for incoming and one for outgoing mail .

To improve speed of access to the web, many ISPs provide a proxy server. This is a computer that stores all the current copies of web pages that have been requested by its customers so that, when another customer requests one, it can return the information more quickly.

Regular traveler?

If you want to be able to dial your ISP at local rates from anywhere in the country, choose one that offers national coverage. Some ISPs, and most online services, have many international points of presence .

ISP OR ONLINE SERVICE?

In the past, your choice of service provider split evenly between basic ISPs (offering email, unlimited access to the internet, and newsgroups), and online services that offered large networks of well organized, authoritative information, members-only email and chat areas, and access to the web.

In recent years, the difference between the two has become less distinct. Many ISPs now offer well-organized gateways to the internet. Apart from content, the main difference between online services and ISPs is cost. Online services generally charge a basic monthly rate that is much lower than many ISPs offer, but is for a fixed number of hours per month. Most ISPs charge a fixed monthly rate for unlimited access.

Web Centers
· **Autos**: New Cars, Used Cars...
· **Bus. & Careers**: Job Listings...
· **Computing**: Screensavers...
· **Entertainment**: TV, Movies...
· **Food**: Recipes, Quick Meals...
· **Games**: Demos, Game Tips...
· **Govt.**: Elections, DMV Forms...
· **Health**: Babies, Conditions...
· **Home & Garden**: Floor Plans...
· **International**: Newspapers...
· **Legal**: Find A Lawyer...
· **Local**: Events, Visitor's Guides...
· **News**: Comics, Crosswords...
· **Personal Finance**: Stocks, Funds...
· **Pictures & Albums**: Galleries...
· **Real Estate**: Homes, Rentals...
· **Research**: Genealogy...
· **Sports**: NBA, Baseball, NASCAR...
· **Travel**: Flights, Hotels...

Channels available
These options are offered by AOL.

57 How a message is sent

23 Choosing a Service Provider

QUESTIONS TO ASK AN ISP

Do you charge a registration or sign-up fee?

What do you charge per month?

Are there any additional charges; e.g. for time online, technical support, software, anything else?

Can I dial up using a number charged at local rate? (Some ISPs offer free calls as part of the package, but these are currently rare.)

Do you offer a free trial?

How many email addresses do you offer? (More than one email address is useful if several family members are to share the email account.)

Do you offer POP3 mail? (This is essential if you want to receive mail on a remote computer.)

Which newsgroups will I be able to access? (Some ISPs offer a limited number of newsgroups, blocking some of those containing adult content.)

What software do you provide?

What customer support/technical support do you offer?

It may be handy to photocopy this page and use it to make notes when you are telephoning different ISPs.

CONNECTING

Once you have chosen your Internet Service Provider, and have either the sign-up software on a CD or all the ISP's details, you are ready to make your first connection to the internet.

USING AN ISP'S SOFTWARE TO CONNECT

If your ISP has provided you with sign-up software, making a connection should be simply a matter of inserting the ISP's CD and following the on-screen instructions.

It is in the interests of ISPs (especially those offering you a free trial period) to make the signing-up procedure as simple, quick, and error-free as possible.

SUPPLYING DETAILS

When you insert the ISP's CD, you will be asked to make a series of choices regarding the installation of software, and to supply some personal details (e.g. your name, age, address, and probably information about hobbies and interests). Unless you are signing up with a "free" ISP you will also probably be asked to supply payment (usually credit card) details.

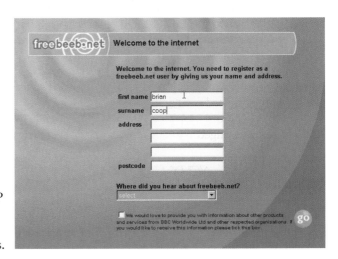

EXPIRATION DATES

Watch the expiration date of free trials! If you gave payment details when you signed up for a free trial, it is usually up to you to cancel the payment if you decide not to continue with the service. Otherwise the monthly amount will be debited from your account once the free trial is over.

USING MORE THAN ONE ISP

On the following pages, we describe how to set up a connection to an ISP using the "dial-up networking" software that is supplied with Windows 98.

This method is particularly recommended if you decide to use (or try out) more than one ISP, because it provides a simple and neat solution.

WHY NEAT?

Prodigy Internet

If you install more than one account you may find that the most recent installation has customized your browser and changed your default email settings. This might be just a cosmetic change, but sometimes the changes affect the default settings for your internet software. The new ISP may set itself up as the connection that launches whenever you open Internet Explorer or Outlook Express and all your email will carry the address connected with that ISP. These settings can be changed

Connection to EZ-ISP

Connection to Bigstores.net

back to your preferred settings, but it can be irritating.

The advantage of using the "dial-up networking" method, which is described on the following pages, is that each connection is kept separate from any other. When you create a dial-up networking "session," it contains all the information relating to a single ISP. Then, whenever you double-click the icon, you are connected to that ISP, leaving your web browser and mail settings unaffected.

CompuServe

WHY USE MORE THAN ONE ISP?

PROS

If you use several ISPs, you reduce the chances of being unable to connect to the net at any time, or send or receive your email. If one ISP's servers are out of action for any reason, you simply dial-up to another ISP and connect to the net by this alternative route. If you have access to any genuinely free ISPs it makes sense to have at least one alternative route to the net.

CONS

If you have too many internet accounts and email addresses, it can become time-consuming to collect your mail. Also, your friends will give up mailing you altogether if you keep sending them new email addresses. One solution to this is to use one mail account only. You can set up Outlook Express to retrieve mail from any POP3 server, regardless of the ISP with which you are connected.

CONNECTING MANUALLY TO YOUR ISP

Before you begin the next steps, it is important to make sure that you have all the necessary information at hand (see box below). Your ISP should supply you with all of these settings.

Finally, with this information at your fingertips, and your modem switched on and connected to an active telephone socket, you are ready to make your first connection to the internet. And this next part is really very easy. Note that the following instructions only apply to the first account that you set up with an ISP. Instructions are given later in the book on how you should go about adding any subsequent accounts.

CONNECTION SETTINGS YOU WILL NEED

• **Your user name and password**
These may be specified by your ISP, or your ISP may have asked you to choose them yourself over the telephone. The important thing is that the user name and password are those that you have agreed with your ISP.

• **Your ISP's phone number**
This is the number you will be dialing to connect to the internet.

• **A second user name and password**
Some ISPs require a second user name to allow you to access your email. Most ISPs require you to have a password different from your main password specifically to allow you to access your incoming email.

• **The ISP's mail server addresses**
There will usually be two of these, one for incoming mail and one for outgoing mail. These addresses will look something like this:
smtp.cdotn.com (*outgoing*)
pop3.cdotn.com (*incoming*)

• **The address of your ISP's news server**
This will be something like this:
news.cdotn.com.

• **Any additional settings**
These may be required by the ISP and are likely to relate to DNS settings and a proxy server. It doesn't matter for now what these settings do, but it is important that you have a note of them right at the start.

1 START CONNECTING

● Double-lick the **Connect to the Internet** icon on your desktop.

2 SET UP MANUALLY

● Check the radio button next to **I want to set up my Internet connection manually...** and click **Next**.

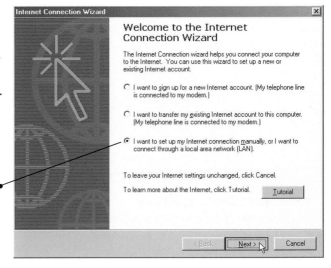

Click the radio button ●

3 USING THE MODEM

● In the next dialog box, check the radio button next to **I connect through a phone line and a modem** and then click **Next**.

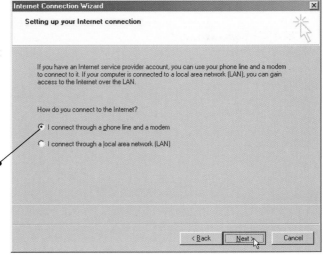

Click the radio button ●

4 TELEPHONE NUMBER

● Type your ISP's telephone number (the one that you have been given for your internet connection) and click **Next**. Ignore the **Advanced…** button for now. If necessary, you can type additional settings later ⬚.

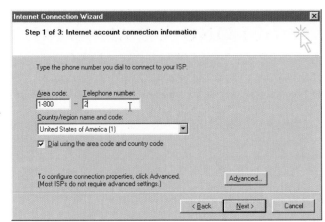

5 USER NAME

● Type your User name, followed by your password, and click on **Next**.

Enter name ●

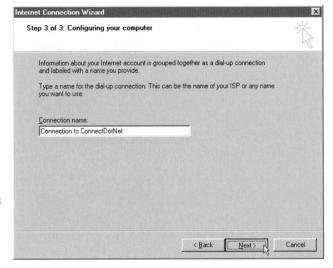

6 IDENTIFY CONNECTION

● Type a name, which can be any text string, to identify the connection. The name is a convenient way to identify the connection and does not affect your dialing-in to your ISP. It is safer just to call this connection the name of your ISP, particularly if you collect a number of accounts. When you have done this, click **Next**.

⬚ **34** **Advanced Connection Settings**

SETTING UP AN EMAIL ACCOUNT

The next few steps relate to setting up your email account. If, for any reason, you don't have all of your email settings at hand (perhaps, for example, you still need to check your POP3 server's address with your ISP) you will be prompted for the same details the first time you try to launch Outlook Express.

1 SETTING UP THE ACCOUNT
● In the next dialog box, click the **Yes** button in answer to **Do you want to set up an Internet account now?** Then click **Next**.

Click Yes ●

2 ENTERING THE NAME
● Type a name in the display box that will appear in the **From** part of your email messages – the name that recipients of your messages will see.

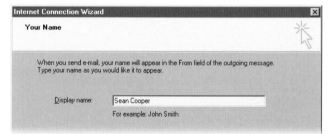

3 ENTERING THE ADDRESS
● Type your email address, as agreed with your ISP.

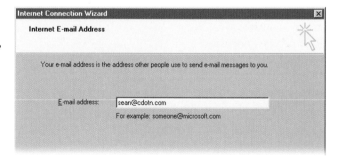

4 ADDING SERVER ADDRESSES

● Type the address for the **Incoming mail (POP3, IMAP or HTTP)** and **Outgoing mail (SMTP) servers**, as supplied by your ISP.

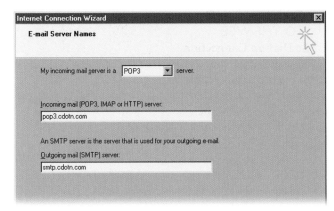

5 ACCOUNT NAME AND PASSWORD

● Type the **Account name** and **Password** required to access your incoming email ⬐. You may choose to click on the **Remember password** box too ⬎.

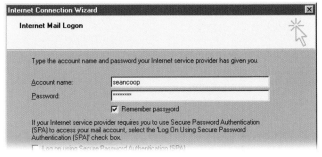

6 MAKING THE CONNECTION

● Check the box **To connect to the internet immediately…** and then click on **Finish** to make a connection to your ISP.

Check here ●

| 28 | **Connection settings you will need** |
| 33 | **Password security** |

7 CONNECTING TO THE WEB

• The **Dial-up Connection** box appears. Type your password if necessary and click **Connect**. You should now be connected to the internet. Double-click the **Internet Explorer** icon on your desktop and watch the web appear on your computer!

PASSWORDS

It is essential that you keep a note of your passwords somewhere private – they may seem memorable at the time, but may not be a year later. (Websites frequently ask you to assign yourself a user name and password to access their content.)

PASSWORD SECURITY

How you use the **Remember password** checkbox, when it appears, is entirely a matter of choice. If you are the only user of your PC then it is a useful feature. It means you don't have to type your password every time you connect to the internet, or collect your email.

If you share your computer with other users, however, you may want to keep certain things password-protected. For example, you may prefer to restrict the access that any children in the household have to certain areas of the internet or to your personal mailbox.

ADVANCED CONNECTION SETTINGS

In many cases you will not need to use any "advanced" settings. They may not be required by your ISP, or may have been set up automatically. The most likely setting you will need to make is to specify that your web browser uses your ISP's proxy server ⌐. This will speed up access to web pages. To do this, follow these steps:

1 INTERNET OPTIONS

• In the Windows 98 **Start** menu choose **Settings** and then **Control Panel.** Now double-click the **Internet Options** icon and click the **Connections** tab.

Internet Options

2 SETTING THE ISP CONNECTION

• On the **Connections** page of the **Internet Properties** dialog box, click the name that identifies the connection to your ISP and click **Settings.**

Select for security check (allows you to turn off sharing – if you have shared folders on your computer – before connecting to the net)

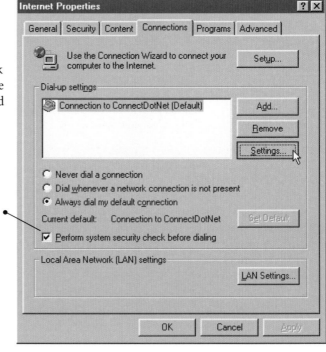

When you are connected

3 USING A PROXY SERVER

● Check the **Use a proxy server** box and in the boxes provided type the **Address** and **Port** number (usually 8080) supplied by your ISP. Then click **OK** to return to the **Internet Properties** dialog box, and click **OK** again.

● The settings you type on the next screen will only affect the dial-up networking session you have highlighted here. (Clearly, this is only relevant if you have accounts with more than one ISP.)

Connection to ConnectDotNet Settings

Automatic configuration

Automatic configuration may override manual settings. To ensure the use of manual settings, disable automatic configuration.

☐ Automatically detect settings

☐ Use automatic configuration script

Address

Proxy server

☑ Use a proxy server

Address: Port:

☐ Bypass proxy server for local addresses

Dial-up settings

User name: cdn43110

Password: ✗✗✗✗✗✗✗✗

Domain: (optional)

Properties

Advanced

☐ Do not allow Internet programs to use this connection

OK   Cancel

CONGRATULATIONS!

Well, that's all the technical stuff over with. Now you are connected, nothing can hold you back – except maybe time and an awareness of telephone charges (if you're unfortunate enough to have to pay them). So get on the web, follow those links, and marvel at the sheer scale of the internet! Once the initial surfing frenzy has worn off, you will soon realize how important it is to organize your time online effectively. How do you do that? Well, knowing exactly what your internet software can do is a useful starting point. Then knowing how to find exactly what you want (and always making a note of the address where you found it) is another great time-saver.

Later in this book you will learn how to start using Internet Explorer ⌐ and Outlook Express ⌐. You will also get an idea of where you can visit to put your new knowledge to immediate effect ▯!

40   **Searching with Internet Explorer**

176   **What Outlook Express Can Do**

37   **What's on the Web?**

ONTO THE WEB

Perhaps the best known aspect of the internet is the World Wide Web. To find your way around it and locate websites, you need to use a web browser and search engines.

WHAT IS A WEB BROWSER?

A web browser is a piece of software installed on your PC that enables you to look at (or "browse") websites. The most popular web browsers are Netscape Navigator and Microsoft Internet Explorer. You can have both of them installed on your PC, and which one you use is a matter of personal preference.

WHICH BROWSER?

The examples shown in this book use Microsoft Internet Explorer, but the pages should look almost the same using Netscape Navigator. New versions of these browsers are released from time to time, adding new features. It is best to use the most recent release of either browser, providing your PC has sufficient memory and processing power to support it.

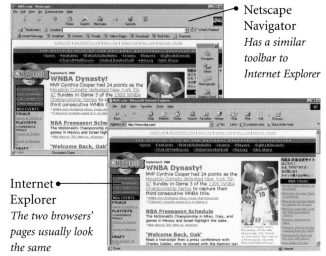

Netscape Navigator
Has a similar toolbar to Internet Explorer

Internet Explorer
The two browsers' pages usually look the same

MORE ABOUT BROWSERS

Two browsers may make the same website look slightly different because they have interpreted the language in which the web pages are written (Hypertext Markup Language or HTML) in a different way.

WHAT'S ON THE WEB?

The World Wide Web is perhaps the best known aspect of the internet. Around the world, computers called servers store pages on websites created by organizations, individuals, and commercial companies, and any computer user who is connected to the internet can access these websites. Some sites exist purely to provide free information, or promote charitable causes, while others offer services or goods for sale, or charge the user to view material, or to play computer games online.

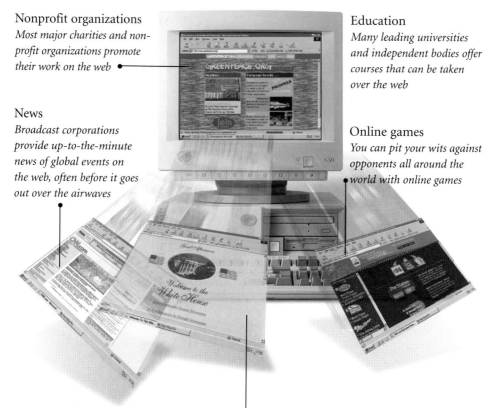

Nonprofit organizations
Most major charities and non-profit organizations promote their work on the web

Education
Many leading universities and independent bodies offer courses that can be taken over the web

News
Broadcast corporations provide up-to-the-minute news of global events on the web, often before it goes out over the airwaves

Online games
You can pit your wits against opponents all around the world with online games

Commercial organizations
You can buy almost anything over the web, from books and clothes to your weekly groceries

Research
Libraries, universities, public and commercial bodies, and individuals all publish information on the web

Government bodies
To email the President or contact your local council, you will almost certainly find the right address on a website

Hobbyists
Individuals create their own websites on topics of interest, but amateur information is not always reliable

WHAT'S ON A WEB PAGE?

In the early days of the web, web pages contained only text and very basic formatting, offering very little in the way of design. Today's web pages are a world away from those of the early pioneers, with many sites aspiring to be multimedia extravaganzas. A web page is likely to incorporate sophisticated graphics, video clips, sound sequences, interactive animations, and miniature software programs known as "applets," on the page.

Download files
Web pages can contain files that you transfer to your own computer to view or install.

Programs
While you are viewing a web page, a program can run independently

Graphics
A well-designed website can be a showcase for the skills of the graphic designer

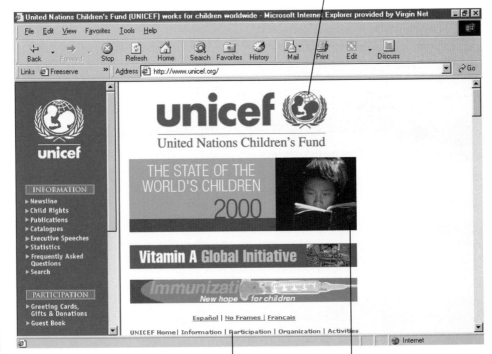

Text
Text within a page can be copied, pasted, and saved to your hard disk

Hypertext links
Use hypertext links, or "hyperlinks," to go directly to other relevant sites

Photographs
Images on a web page can also act as hyperlinks

Multimedia files
These can be sound, video, or interactive animations

50 **Downloading from the Internet**

How a Web Page Works

Web pages are built using a computer language called HyperText Markup Language (HTML). HTML comprises a set of tags that identify the elements on a web page as being of a certain type – for example, text, image, or multimedia file. The HTML tags tell the web browser where to find the files to build the page, how to display them, and the tags act as the glue that binds the files together.

Browser window
This is how the web page appears in the browser window •

HTML tag
This line tells the browser that the file is a HyperText Markup document •

HTML code
This code tells the browser how to display a web page. HTML instructions are known as "tags." View the code of a page by choosing "View Source" in your web browser •

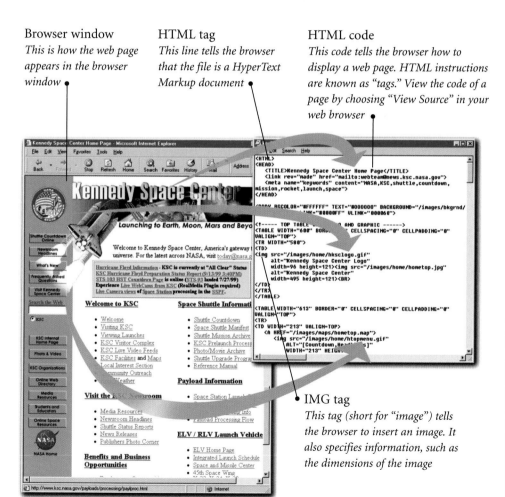

IMG tag
This tag (short for "image") tells the browser to insert an image. It also specifies information, such as the dimensions of the image

SEARCHING WITH INTERNET EXPLORER

Searching the web for information is undoubtedly one of the most common things you will do online. Unless you look for a known web address 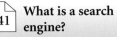, you will use a collection of programs and free services commonly known as "search engines."

1 CLICK SEARCH
● Click the **Search** button on the Toolbar. A frame will appear in the left of your browser window.

2 SEARCH CATEGORY
● Type a search term in the search text box and click on **Search**.
● Note that there is a **Customize** button in this frame. Clicking on this allows you to choose the categories of search available and which search engines 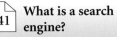 you wish to use.

3 LIST OF HITS
● When the list of hits appears in the left-hand frame, hold the mouse pointer over any entry to see the address and a brief description of the website. Click any entry to display that site in the main part of the browser window.

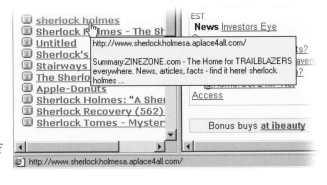

42 Using a Web Address

41 What is a search engine?

WHAT IS A SEARCH ENGINE?

There are two types of search engine: the *search index* is a vast catalog made up of every word taken from all the web pages searched by a program called a "bot" or spider, which crawls through the web and returns its information to the index; the *web directory* is compiled by real people who organize web pages into categories and subcategories, allowing you to search very effectively. The most popular search engines now combine both principles. Your web browser will connect to search engines to seek information, but you can also go directly to a search engine's website (using its web address ☐) to take advantage of more advanced features. The screen below is from the Yahoo! website.

Enter a search term here and click on the **Search** *button* •

The advanced search option is recommended for greater relevance in your results •

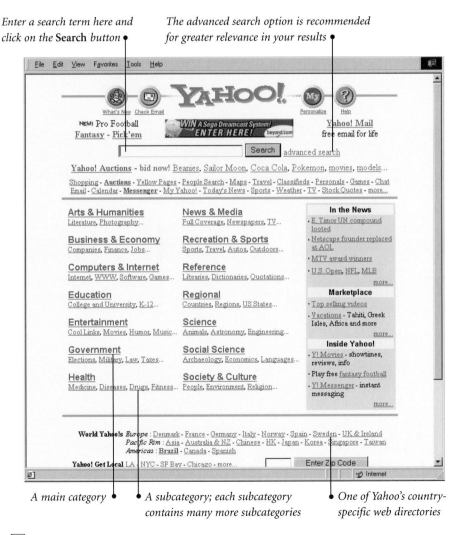

A main category • *A subcategory; each subcategory contains many more subcategories* *One of Yahoo's country-specific web directories*

        Using a
 42 Web address

USING A WEB ADDRESS

Website addresses are now a common sight in magazines, on products, and at the end of television and radio programs. If you know the address of the website that you want to visit, your web browser will take you straight to it if you simply type this address in the address bar at the top of the screen.

1 CLEARING THE ADDRESS BAR

● Before you can type in a new address, you must first clear the current contents. Position the cursor anywhere in the address field and click once.
● The contents of the address bar are highlighted.
● Press the `← Bksp` key to delete the contents.

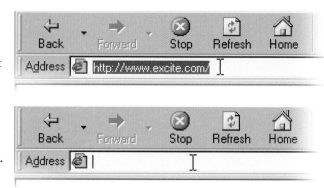

2 TYPING THE ADDRESS

● Now type the full address, taking care to copy exactly all the spelling and punctuation.

3 CONNECTING TO THE SITE

● Once you have typed the address, click on the **Go** button to the right of the address or press the `Enter ←` key. Once the connection is made, the web page will start to appear on your screen.

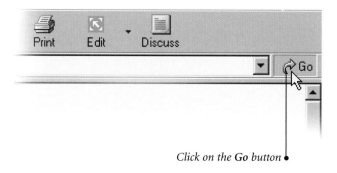

Click on the Go button ●

BROWSING THE WEB OFFLINE

Offline browsing is a very useful feature that enables you to store web pages or even an entire website on your hard drive. This is especially useful if you wish to spend time browsing a site without tying up the telephone line or running up unnecessary connection charges (if you have to pay them). It can also be of use if you wish to read certain websites on a portable computer while traveling, since an internet connection is obviously not required while browsing offline. You can specify websites for offline browsing when you use the **Add to Favorites** feature.

To browse offline, choose **Work Offline** from the **File** menu.

1 CHOOSING THE PAGE
● From the web page you wish to save for offline browsing, choose **Add to Favorites** from the **Favorites** menu.

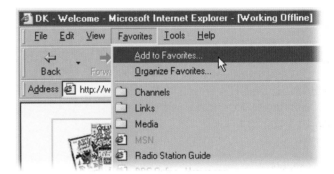

2 MAKING THE PAGE AVAILABLE
● In the **Add Favorite** dialog box, tick the check box next to **Make available offline**.
● Then click **Customize…**

Check box for offline browsing options

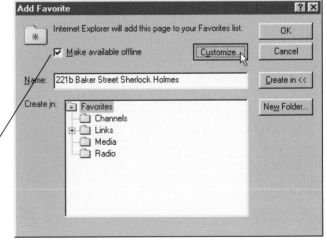

3 USING THE WIZARD

● Now follow the instructions in the **Offline Favorite Wizard**.

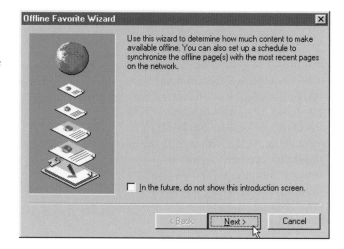

Advanced Options

You can nominate any Favorite for offline browsing by right-clicking it in the Favorites list. If you have already nominated a Favorite for offline browsing, you can start the synchronization process by right-clicking it and choosing **Synchronize** from the drop-down menu.

WHAT CAN I ACCESS OFFLINE?

Next time you are working offline, start your browser and look at your Favorites list. You can view any pages offline that appear in bold type. Entries that are grayed out will be unavailable offline. The shape of the mouse pointer will indicate whether or not a page is available.

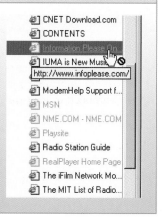

4 UNAVAILABLE WEB PAGES

● If you click a link that is unavailable offline, the **Web page unavailable while offline** dialog box will appear, giving the option to connect to your ISP.

DO A LITTLE RESEARCH

The **Offline Favorite Wizard** asks you how many "links deep" you wish to download from the page you have chosen for offline browsing. It is worth exploring the site a little before deciding what is a sensible setting for this box. If you choose to save links two levels deep without checking things out first, you may inadvertently save some very large, unwanted files to your hard drive.

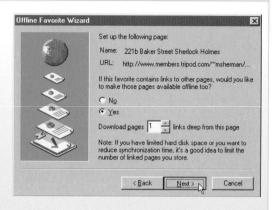

SYNCHRONIZING PAGES

To keep the web pages that you have stored on your computer up to date, your browser will need to visit the appropriate sites to update the pages while you are online. This process is known as synchronizing the pages.

WHEN TO SYNCHRONIZE
You can specify how often this is done, and at what time of day. Unless you need to synchronize a large number of offline pages, your browser can perform this task in the background while you are browsing the web. To manage these tasks, choose **Synchronize** from the Tools menu and type the relevant settings in the **Items to Synchronize** dialog box.

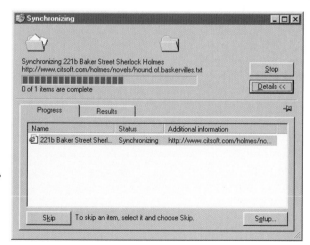

The synchronization process is shown above.

MULTIMEDIA ON THE WEB

Over the last five years, web pages have come alive with animations, sounds, a host of multimedia effects, and ever more ingenious interactive elements.

The introduction of new technologies such as Java and ActiveX, applications like RealPlayer and Shockwave, and significant enhancements to HTML (the "tagged" language in which web pages are written), have brought exciting new multimedia capabilities and levels of interactivity to the web.

LIVE ON THE WEB

Multimedia applications still do not run as smoothly as they would from a CD or DVD-ROM (unless you have a state-of-the-art internet connection), but the performance of web-based multimedia improves almost monthly; unlike the CD-ROM, the web can deliver "live" TV and radio broadcasts.

USING INTERNET EXPLORER

Internet Explorer is capable of handling most of the multimedia file types that appear on web pages, but some pages contain files that will not "run" without additional software called a "plug-in." You can download new plug-ins or upgrade existing ones from the developers' sites, from specialized software sites, or from the CDs that come with computer magazines. You will know if a web page requires a particular plug-in because it will tell you so.

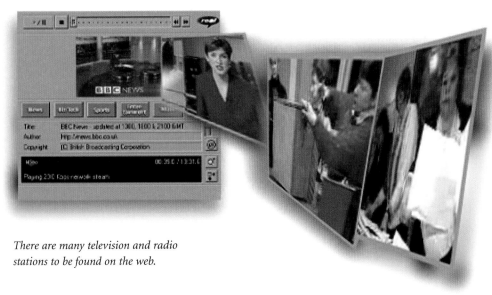

There are many television and radio stations to be found on the web.

DOWNLOADING THE NECESSARY SOFTWARE

If your browser meets a file type that it doesn't know how to handle, you will be given the option to download the relevant software, or "plug-in," to enable you to continue viewing that page. If you agree to download the software, you are usually taken to the home page for the maker of that plug-in to find out more about it before deciding whether you want to proceed ⬚.

RADIO

As well as internet-only radio stations, many national and local stations broadcast live over the internet. These will run in the background while you browse the web. Internet Explorer's Radio Guide provides links to many radio stations.

THE RADIO TOOLBAR

● To access the radio Toolbar, choose **Toolbars** from the **View** menu and then **Radio** from the drop-down menu.

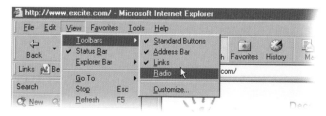

● From the **Radio** toolbar, choose **Radio Station Guide** from the **Radio Stations** drop-down menu. Many links to radio stations are provided on this page, arranged by country, region, or category.

⬚ **Downloading From the Internet** 50

ONLINE GAMING

The internet has a lot to offer the computer games enthusiast. For a start, producers of commercial games software have their own sites, which contain, for example, news, upgrades, competitions, and special offers. But these are far outnumbered by the sites offering hints, cheats, and links to virtually every computer game ever produced. These pages are created by the games' players – with an enthusiasm and devotion sometimes verging on the fanatical!

MULTIPLAYER

Many games today have multiplayer online capabilities. If you have a working modem plugged in and ready to go, you can use a menu within such games to gain access automatically to servers on the internet on which the game is being played. For an excellent list of online games visit ⬚:
http://directory.hotbot. com/games/.

SOLO GAMES, PUZZLES, AND TRIVIA

The crossword puzzle on this site is changed daily. Click on any of the squares to highlight the appropriate across or down entry; then type the solution. If you want to change your entry, you can simply overtype it.

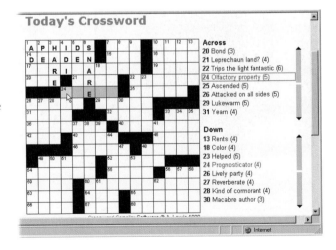

GAMES ROOMS

If you prefer playing against a real opponent, join one of the many games rooms on the internet.

The MSN Gaming Zone offers a selection of games. Go to **zone.msn.com** and click **Game Index** in the left-hand margin.

Below is an example of a backgammon game.

Chat with your opponent by typing in this box •

• *Drag and drop the counters to move them*

• *Click on the dice to "roll" them when it is your turn*

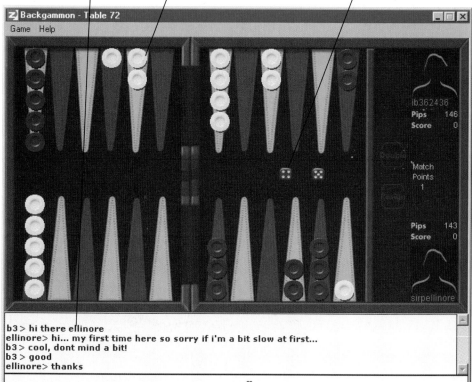

b3 > hi there ellinore
ellinore> hi... my first time here so sorry if i'm a bit slow at first...
b3 > cool, dont mind a bit!
b3 > good
ellinore> thanks

DOWNLOADING FROM THE INTERNET

The internet is full of free stuff – books, help files, sound and video clips, photographs, screen-savers, software, lists of links to free stuff, and so on. In fact, you can download the images from any web page you visit simply by right-clicking the image and choosing **Save Picture as…** from the drop-down menu.

WHAT IS FREEWARE?

Copyright exists as much on the internet as anywhere else. But there are thousands of things that are absolutely free for you to download, keep, and use.

Downloading software from the web is easy. You will usually click a download button on the web page, or a link that begins the process for you. The installer file in this example was found on **www.download.com.**

Freeware only
The instructions on these pages relate only to the downloading of "free" software.

1 CLICKING TO DOWNLOAD
● The item that you are wishing to download should have a **Download** button. Click on this.

RealJukebox Basic *new popular pick*

- Download Now
- Developer's Site

- All Downloa
- Product Spe

2 SAVING THE PROGRAM
● When the **File Download** dialog box appears, ensure the **Save this program to disk** option is checked and click **OK**.

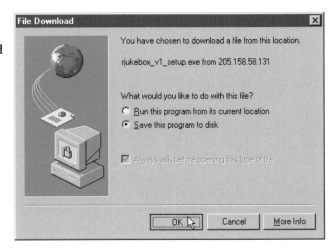

3 CHOOSING A LOCATION

● In the **Save As** dialog box, choose a location to save the file. (In this example, the file will be saved in a folder called **downloads.**) Then click on **Save**.

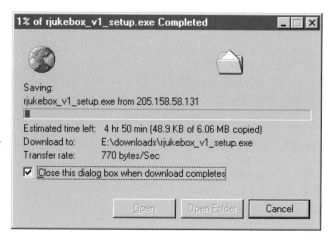

4 MONITORING AND INSTALLING

● A window will then appear showing the progress of the downloading.

● When the file has finished downloading, you will need to open the folder in which you saved it and double-click the file. The software's installation program should then take care of the rest of the installation.

● It is best to carry out the installation after you have finished your online session, because installation may require you to restart your computer, thereby ending your online session. Some programs run the installation process automatically, simply prompting you for information or a click on a proceed button. This is often the case for self-installing browser plug-ins.

SHAREWARE AND FREEWARE

Shareware is software that is free to try for a limited period. When the time is up you should pay up or stop using it! It is increasingly common for shareware to time itself out at the end of the trial period. Freeware is software that you can keep and use, but is still protected by copyright.

Public domain software is free, and may be altered and used for profit. But the author has to state explicitly that it is public domain. Registering any software can bring many benefits – free upgrades, documentation, extra features, and the knowledge that you are funding further software.

NEWSGROUPS

Newsgroups on the internet are rarely concerned with "news" in the sense of current affairs. They are essentially public email discussion forums devoted to a wide range of topics and interests.

USING NEWSGROUPS

Newsgroups provide a forum for people to discuss topics of mutual interest and share information – whether highly technical or just gossip. They can be excellent places to get advice if, for example, you have a computer problem. Participants (or "subscribers," to use the correct term) "post" messages to be seen and be responded to, either publicly or privately, by any reader of that newsgroup.

A WEALTH OF INFORMATION

When you connect to a particular news server and download the full list of available newsgroups, you can scroll through the list and choose to view any that interest you.

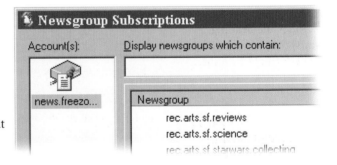

WHAT IS USENET?

Usenet is the name given to the large body of newsgroups (there are currently more than 30,000 of them) distributed around the world by computers known as news servers. These servers exchange information so that each one carries a copy of the most recent messages. Usenet is not, strictly speaking, part of the internet, although internet sites are used to carry its newsgroups.

Most ISPs provide access to Usenet newsgroups, usually via their own news servers.

SETTING UP OUTLOOK EXPRESS AS A NEWSREADER

If Outlook Express has not been set up as a newsreader you will need to do this in order to access the newsgroups.

Remember that you need to be online to download the newsgroups, and this may take ten minutes or so.

1 ACCESSING THE DEFAULT PAGE

● Access the default Outlook Express page by clicking **Outlook Express** at the top of the **Folders** panel.

2 SETTING UP AN ACCOUNT

● Under the heading **Newsgroups** click on **Set up a Newsgroups account...**.

3 ENTERING NEWS SERVER NAME

● The Internet Connection Wizard will now appear. The easy set-up procedure is very similar to that described for setting up an email account 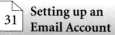, but here you need to type the name of your news server as provided by your ISP.

● You will now be given the option to download all available newsgroups.

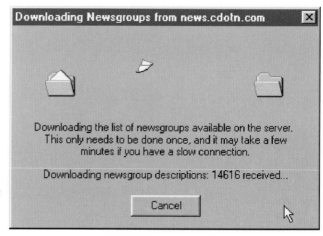

<table>
<tr><td>31</td><td>Setting up an Email Account</td></tr>
</table>

READING MESSAGES IN A NEWSGROUP

The **Newsgroup Subscriptions** window shows the name of the news server in the left panel and the names of newsgroups available to you in the main panel on the right. You are now ready to read messages from your chosen newsgroup.

1 NEWSGROUPS SUBSCRIPTIONS

- To view the **Newsgroup Subscriptions** window, choose **Newsgroups** from the Tools menu.

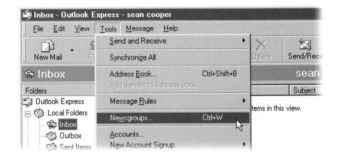

2 LOCATING A NEWSGROUP

- To locate a chosen newsgroup, type a key word in the **Display newsgroups which contain:** box.

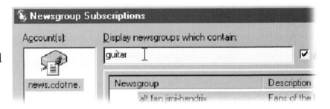

3 VIEWING A GROUP

- To view the contents of a group, click the name in the list and click the **Subscribe** button.

4 DOWNLOADING A MESSAGE

- To download a message, simply double-click on it.

POSTING TO A NEWSGROUP

The procedure for posting a message to a newsgroup is basically the same as sending an email to a friend. The only real difference is that your words will be published for all the newsgroup's subscribers to read.

1 HIGHLIGHTING A MESSAGE
● Highlight the message to which you wish to reply. Click the **Reply Group** button.

2 ENTERING YOUR REPLY
● Type your reply into the email reply window that appears, and click **Send.**

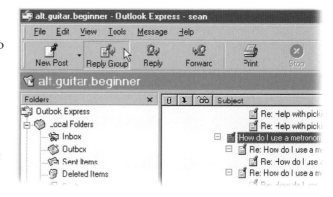

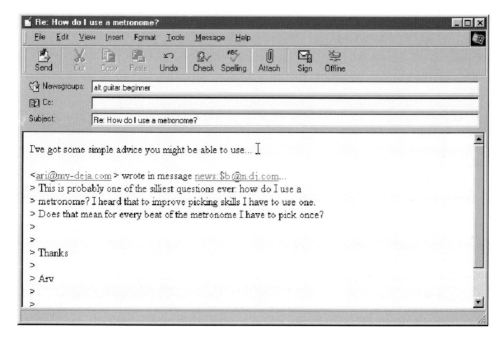

EMAIL AND CHAT

For many people, electronic mail is one of the most important reasons for getting connected to the internet. For full details of how to use Outlook Express, see Section 4 on page 174.

USING EMAIL

With an email software program, you can write letters on your PC, address them to the destination email address, and send them winging their way around the globe in a matter of moments. You can also enclose images and even video clips.

SIGNING UP
When you sign up for a new internet account, you will receive one or more unique email addresses. Outlook Express, which is supplied as part of Windows 98, contains an email client program that enables you both to send and receive email.

Speed is relative
Although email can be lightning fast, your mail might as well be delivered by mule if the recipient doesn't check the mail! Email can only be delivered when the recipient requests new mail from the server.

ADVANTAGES AND DISADVANTAGES OF EMAIL

ADVANTAGES OF EMAIL
There are many advantages to using email rather than conventional mail. First, it is cheap – never usually costing more than the price of a local phone call to send. Secondly, it is very fast. If all connections are working effectively, an email message can be received by the addressee within minutes of your sending the message, regardless of location. You can also "attach" files to your email messages (for example, documents, spreadsheets, photographs, and sound clips).

DISADVANTAGES OF EMAIL
Email is less private than conventional mail since its contents could be read by anyone with access to your, or the recipient's, computer. It is therefore wise not to send anything too sensitive via email unless you have some way of protecting the contents – by using encryption software, for instance. For more information on secure email, refer to **Sending secure messages** in the Outlook Express **Help** file).

GET THE ADDRESS RIGHT

It is especially important with electronic mail that you get the address absolutely right. Unlike conventional mail, there isn't a local mailman who can use some judgment if an address is nearly right.

Email is entirely mechanical, so "nearly right" is simply wrong. Any wrongly addressed mail will be automatically returned to sender (or "bounced back" as it is otherwise known) with a "failed to deliver" message from the remote server.

THE ELEMENTS THAT MAKE UP AN EMAIL ADDRESS

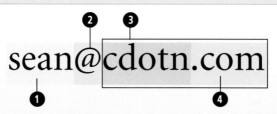

❶ User Name
Identifies the addressee.
❷ Separator
An @ ("at") symbol separates the user and domain names.
❸ Domain name
Is the computer address, with periods separating the parts.

❹ Suffix
*The suffix **com** indicates a commercial organization based in the US. A company based in the UK would more commonly end with **co.uk**, although **com** and **net** are also frequently used. Other suffixes include **gov** for a*

*government organization, and **edu** or **ac** for an academic institution. All countries except the US also add an extra two-letter suffix. For the United Kingdom this is **uk**, **il** is for Israel, and **nz** is the New Zealand suffix.*

HOW A MESSAGE IS SENT

When you have addressed and sent your message it is sent to your ISP's outgoing (SMTP) mail server. From here it is forwarded to the appropriate ISP. When it arrives at the ISP in the address, it is delivered to the recipient's "pigeon-hole." The next time the addressee checks his or her mail (by logging on to the ISP's POP3 server) the mail is delivered.

EMAIL ON THE MOVE

It is very useful to have more than one email account so that you can read messages on the move. Web-based email accounts are useful because you can log on to them via a secure website from any computer with an internet connection and retrieve and send mail. Microsoft offers a service called Hotmail (you can sign up for an account from the opening screen of Outlook Express), and Yahoo offers a similar service (visit **www.yahoo.com** for information).

A word of warning, however. The more accounts you have, the longer it will take to trawl through them all to see if you have any messages.

CHAT ROOMS

To chat with other internet users, you need a chat "client" program and an internet chat "room" to use it in. These are available on a number of websites and will allow you to have "conversations" with all manner of people from all over the world. You will have the option of speaking to everyone in the room or, should you prefer, talking one-to-one with another visitor to the chat room.

WHAT TO DISCUSS?

Chat is currently big on the web, with many websites offering moderated chat areas where you can meet other users to gossip, flirt, argue, chat, and maybe even discuss whatever the site was set up to discuss! Some sites – especially those belonging to broadcasting and media companies – may provide "celebrity" chat sessions giving visitors the opportunity to put questions to authors, rock stars, politicians, and so on. These are regular features of the online services, available to subscribers.

By entering our rooms, you agree to abide by our CHAT R

Handle	sean
Email Address:	(optio
Chat Room:	The Net Cafe ▼
Line Count:	30

No Frames ▼   Enter Chat Room

Entering the chat room
This image shows someone logging in to a chat site.
The user's "handle" need not be his or her real name.

CHILDREN AND CHAT ROOMS

The dangers for children in chat rooms include exposure to unacceptable subjects, getting involved in abusive conversations, and encountering adults masquerading as children. To counter these problems: Don't leave children completely alone when they are on-line; get to know who they are chatting with; make sure they don't give out personal details that could identify them; and tell them never to meet people from a chat room without your permission.

CHAT SET-UP

Chat is becoming increasingly easy to set up and use on the web. Some sites require you to download and install a plug-in 🗋 to participate. You may also be asked to fill in a registration form. Others require no configuration or plug-ins – you simply go to the web page and join in.

Connecting to a chat room is easy. All you need to do is choose a user name, type in your email address, and wait briefly before entering the lobby.

In the early days of the net, Internet Relay Chat (IRC) was the most widely used chat medium. It is still very popular, but seems bewilderingly fast to a beginner.

The screen shown on this page is typical of most chat client programs, allowing you to read the conversation and compose your reply on the same screen.

The main panel shows the ongoing "public" conversation. All users of the room are listed in this panel. Double-click any user's name to speak privately to him or her (you can never really be sure)

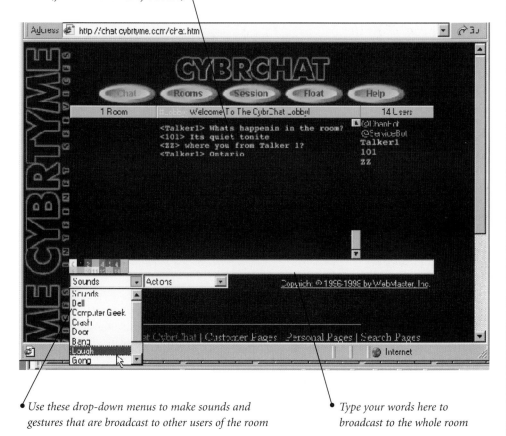

Use these drop-down menus to make sounds and gestures that are broadcast to other users of the room

Type your words here to broadcast to the whole room

47 **Downloading the necessary software**

CHATTING IN 3D WORLDS

Online 3D chat environments fall somewhere between online games, chat areas, and virtual communities.

In some of these multi-user environments you can actually build your own virtual dwelling, trade, and take part in competitions as well as chatting with the other online "residents." The example shown here – Microsoft's V-Chat – offers a typical 3D chat environment. When you first run V-Chat you are

asked to choose a user name and an avatar to represent you. An avatar is the 3D figure that will represent you. You can use

it to move around the chat zones and to display a range of gestures and facial expressions to the group to which you are talking.

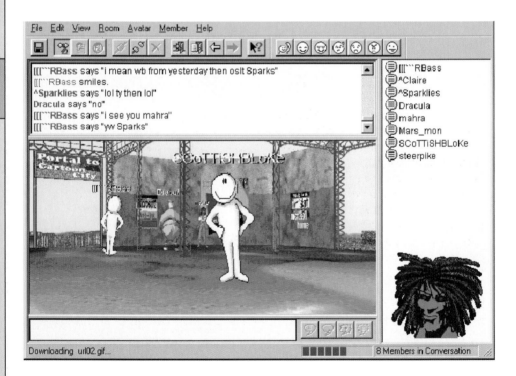

EMOTICONS AND ABBREVIATIONS

As your experience of sending and receiving email grows, you may notice strange punctuation symbols in some messages that you read. These are called "emoticons" (emotional icons) and they are used in email and other electronic communications to convey humor and emotion in a typed medium where it can be easy to misinterpret the intention and tone of what is being said. Emoticons resemble facial expressions when viewed with your head tilted to the left. Here are some of the more common emoticons and abbreviations and what they mean.

: -)	Happy	AFAIK	As far as I know
: -))	Very happy	BRB	Be right back
: - (	Sad	BTW	By the way
: - ((	Very sad	CUL or CUL8R	See you later
: - /	Undecided	FAQ	Frequently asked question
: - p	Tongue-in-cheek		
: - *	Kissing	IMO	In my opinion
: - t	Angry	LOL	Laughing out loud
: - V	Shouting	OIC	Oh I see
: - O	Shocked	ROTFLOL	Rolling on the floor laughing out loud
: - {	Disapproving		
; -)	Winking	THK	Thanks

NETIQUETTE

When you communicate in the internet's public spaces – newsgroups, chatrooms, online games, 3D virtual worlds, and so on – you need to observe certain codes of behavior. Much of this is common sense and everyday courtesy. Just remember that there is a real person at the other end of the line and you won't go far wrong. Here is some basic advice to follow:

• When you first enter a chat room, lurk for a while, read the messages, get a feel for the sort of discussions and the general style of conversation in the room. With newsgroups, it is very important that you read the frequently asked questions (FAQ) file for the group. If you ask a question that features prominently in the FAQ, you will not endear yourself to the regular users of the group.

• Don't SHOUT– typing in capital letters is known as shouting. It is universally disliked because blocks of text in capitals are hard to read.
• Be careful with humor – it can be difficult to convey humor or irony in a written form without giving offense – if you make a comment that you think might be ambiguous in tone, back it up with an emoticon.

BROWSING THE WEB

ROWSING THE WEB is an easy-to-follow guide to Microsoft's Web-browsing program, Internet Explorer. This section of the Essential Internet Guide is for people with very little experience of using this program. Internet Explorer's essential features, from launching the program and understanding the screen and toolbars to personalizing Internet Explorer to meet your particular needs, are presented in separate chapters to allow easy understanding of their functions.

INTERNET EXPLORER

Internet Explorer is one of the most popular web-browsing programs and offers all the facilities that you need to browse the web and become part of the online community.

LAUNCHING INTERNET EXPLORER

You can launch Internet Explorer directly from your computer's desktop or from the Windows Start menu by following the instructions below. Before you can actually connect to a website using Explorer you will need to connect to your Internet Service Provider. It does not matter whether you do this before or after starting Explorer. When Explorer starts running, it checks to see if it can find an active internet connection. If it can't find a connection it will usually prompt you to make a connection. If Explorer is unable to make an automatic connection for any reason, you do not have to close the program and start again. You can connect manually to your service provider at any time while Explorer is running.

CONNECT TO YOUR SERVICE PROVIDER

- If you are using a dial-up connection, click on your Service Provider's dial-up networking connection and double-click.
- In the **Connect To** dialog box, type your user name and password.
- Click once on the **Connect** button to dial your Service Provider.

1 USING THE START MENU

- Click on **Start** on the Windows taskbar to bring up the main menu.
- Highlight **Programs**, and move across to highlight **Internet Explorer** on the pop-up menu that appears.
- Click on **Internet Explorer** and the Explorer window opens .

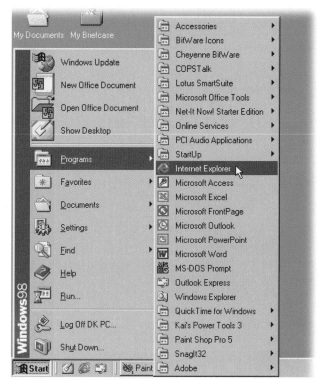

2 USING A SHORTCUT

- Alternatively, locate the Internet Explorer shortcut on your desktop. This is a blue, graphically styled "e" with **Internet** written beneath it.
- Position the mouse over it and double-click to launch Internet Explorer.
- The Explorer window appears .

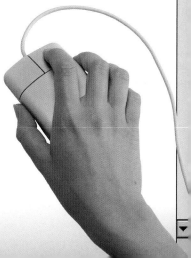

The Explorer Window

THE EXPLORER WINDOW

The Explorer main browser window opens automatically when you start Internet Explorer. It offers a selection of different toolbars, including a standard menu bar, an area for viewing web pages and a status bar at the foot of the window. The status bar displays information relating to the transfer of pages and connectivity.

THE EXPLORER WINDOW

1 Title bar
The Title bar shows the title of the current web page. It also tells you whether you are connected to the internet or are working offline.

2 Menu bar
This shows the main menus that give you access to all Explorer's features.

3 Standard buttons
This toolbar contains all the main features you need to navigate around the web.

4 Address bar
This is where you type the addresses of websites that you want to visit.

5 Links bar
This toolbar provides a selection of links to Microsoft-related websites.

6 Main browsing window
This area is where the websites that you visit will be displayed.

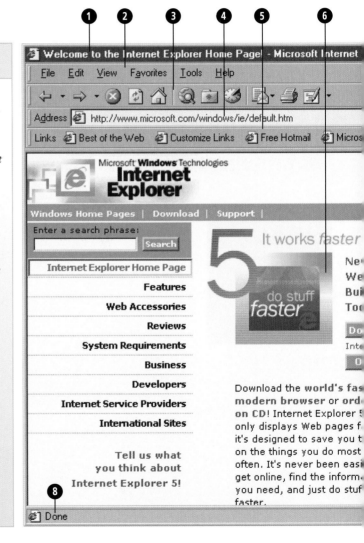

Using the
72 Address Field

CROWDED TOOLBAR?

You can hide the labels on the Standard toolbar to make room for more buttons. Right-click on the toolbar and click **Customize** in the menu. In the **Text options** box of the **Customize** window, click the arrow and select **No text labels**. Click on **Close**.

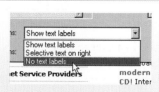

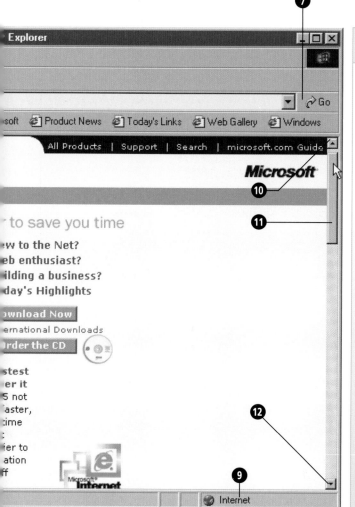

THE EXPLORER WINDOW

7 Go button 🗋
After typing the address of a website, using this button will request the page.

8 Status bar
This bar has information relating to the activity being carried out. For example, "Done" indicates that a requested web page has been transferred to your web browser, or, if you click on a hyperlink 🗋, the URL of that link will be displayed.

9 Connectivity icon
When you are working online, this icon is displayed.

10 Scroll-up arrow
Click on this arrow to move up the current web page.

11 Scroll bar box
Drag this box in the scroll bar to see other parts of the current page quickly.

12 Scroll-down arrow
Click on this arrow to move down the current web page.

73 **Connecting to a site**

75 **Recognizing hypertext links**

THE EXPLORER TOOLBARS

It is perfectly possible to use Internet Explorer using only the features provided on the standard buttons toolbar. This toolbar is at the top of the Explorer window and comprises a row of graphically styled buttons. These buttons are shortcuts to features that will help you find your way round the web quickly, so it is worth spending time familiarizing yourself with the toolbar and learning what each symbol means. Each item on the toolbar is also in the main menus.

THE STANDARD TOOLBAR

❶ Back 📄
Takes you to the previous page you were on.
❷ Forward
Displays the page on screen before using the Back button.
❸ Stop
Stops a page downloading.

❹ Refresh
Refreshes the current page to show the latest version.
❺ Home
Loads the default home page.
❻ Search 📄
Opens the Search panel in the Explorer window. This gives you

access to features that help you connect to search engines.
❼ Favorites 📄
Opens the Favorites panel in the Explorer window, which allows you to create, access, and manage your favorite sites on the web.

77	Navigating Back and Forth
108	Searching the Internet
82	The Favorites Panel

CUSTOMIZING A TOOLBAR

You might want to move the toolbars. To move the **Links** toolbar, place the cursor over the "handle," hold down the mouse button, the cursor becomes a double-headed arrow, then "drag" the bar to the preferred location.

ScreenTips

If you forget what any of the buttons on the toolbar do, all you have to do is click on the button and wait for a few seconds. A box appears with the button's name.

THE STANDARD TOOLBAR

❽ History ▯

Opens the History panel to the left in the Explorer window. This provides a list of websites that you have previously visited when using Explorer and by clicking one you can automatically connect to it.

❾ Mail

Provides a menu of options related to email. These include opening a new email message and pasting the address of the current page into a new message.

❿ Print

Prints the current page.

⓫ Edit

Allows you to edit the code of the current web page, either in text form or using a web page editor, such as FrontPage. Save any changes on your hard disk, but they will not affect the web page itself.

▯ **Using the**
79 **Browsing History**

SAVING CONTENT

It is not possible for you to create or alter web pages using the Internet Explorer browser. However, there will be many occasions when you come across screens containing information that you want to save, review later on, or to edit for your own personal use. Internet Explorer enables you to save text, images, and other files and programs onto your hard disk. Open a web page that you would like to save for later use, and try some of the techniques described here.

1 SAVING A WEB PAGE

● To save an entire web page to your hard disk, click on **File** in the menu bar and select **Save As**.
● In the **Save Web Page** dialog box, type the file name and click on **Save**.

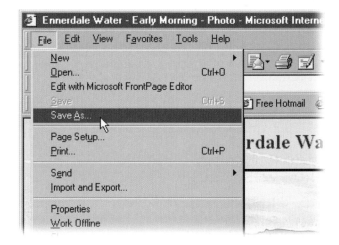

SAVING IMAGES AS WALLPAPER

If you see a striking image on a web page, you can use Explorer to set it as your Windows wallpaper. Follow Step 2 (opposite), but choose **Save As Wallpaper** from the pop-up menu.

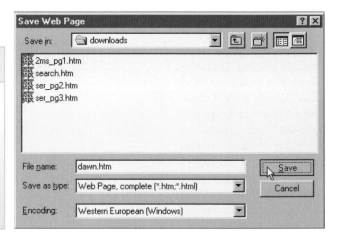

2 SAVING IMAGES

● Place the mouse cursor on the image that you want to save. Click the right mouse button to display a pop-up menu.

● Select **Save Picture As** and click with the left mouse button.

● In the **Save Picture** dialog box, navigate to the folder where you would like to save the file.

● Type a name in the **File name** box and click on the **Save** button.

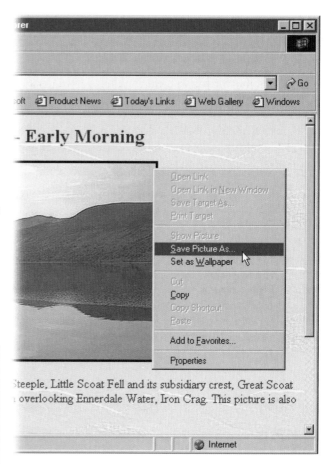

DOWNLOADING FROM WEB PAGES

Many web pages contain files such as multimedia sound or video files, PDF files (Portable Document Files that can be viewed using Acrobat Reader), or computer programs. It is usually possible to save these files onto your hard disk. To save a file, follow Step 2 above and on the pop-up menu choose **Save Target As**, which will be "live" on the menu. You'll need the right software to view or play the files that you save.

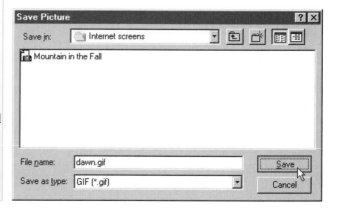

MOVING BETWEEN PAGES

Browsing, or "surfing," the web is simply a process of opening a web page in your browser, identifying the "hot" elements on that page and using them to move to another page.

USING THE ADDRESS FIELD

When you connect to your Internet Service Provider ⃞ and start Internet Explorer, your default home page ⃞ automatically opens in the browser window ⃞. This page is likely to be a Microsoft page or the home page of your service provider. While it may contain useful information for new users, soon you will want to strike out and visit a site of your choice, perhaps your company's website or an international news site. You do this by telling your computer the address of the site you wish to visit. Find the addresses of several sites you would like to visit and try accessing them following the instructions below.

1 CLEARING THE ADDRESS BAR
● Before you can type the address of a site you must first clear the current contents of the address bar. Position the mouse cursor anywhere in the address field and click once.
● The contents of the address bar are highlighted.
● Press the ⃞← Bksp⃞ key to delete the contents.

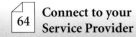
64 Connect to your Service Provider

99 Changing your Home Page

66 The Explorer Window

2 TYPING THE ADDRESS

You will notice that there is now a flashing insertion point in the address bar, ready for you to begin typing. Type the address as it appears, taking care to copy exactly all the punctuation and spelling.

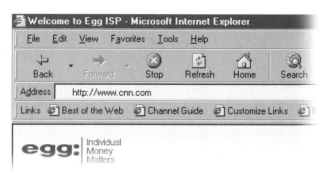

3 CONNECTING TO A SITE

Once you have typed the address, move the mouse cursor over the **Go** button, to the right of the address bar, and click once. Alternatively, you can also press the [Enter ⏎] key. Wait for a few moments while your computer contacts the remote computer you are calling. You can follow the progress of this call by watching the information in the Status bar at the foot of the browser window. Once the connection has been made, you will see the information in your browser window begin to change. When the Status bar says **Done**, the page has been fully downloaded to your computer.

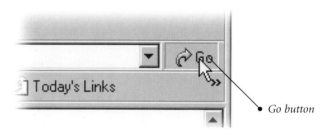

• *Go button*

4 EDITING AN ADDRESS

If you mistype the address or get it wrong, don't worry. Just as you can with a word processor, you can simply edit your mistakes.

● Position the mouse cursor after the character you wish to change and click the mouse button once. This will highlight the entire address, as in Step 1.

● Click again and the cursor will change to a flashing cursor ready for you to type any changes using the keyboard.

● When the address is correct, either click on the **Go** button or press Enter ⏎.

HAVING TROUBLE CONNECTING?

ⓘ The page cannot be displayed

The page you are looking for is currently unavailable. The Web site might be experiencing technical difficulties, or you may need to adjust your browser settings.

There is a wide variety of reasons why you may experience difficulty connecting to a site. Servers sometimes go down and cannot be accessed. If you cannot get connected for this reason wait before trying again, but the wait can be anything from a few seconds to several hours. Another reason may be that you have mistyped the address. Check that the spelling and punctuation are correct and that no extra characters have crept in. Any slight discrepancy will prevent a connection.

FOLLOWING LINKS BETWEEN PAGES

Links are the very essence of the World Wide Web, and it is by following them that you can move from page to page without typing a new address each time. Links have several different guises, and learning to recognize their various forms will help you get the most from the web. Hypertext links are the most common form and are displayed as text on the page, but graphic buttons and other images are increasingly used as a way of encouraging you to move to another page. Dorling Kindersley's website uses both types of links. Try identifying each of the types of links described here and following them using the instructions below.

RECOGNIZING HYPERTEXT LINKS

These are the most common and easily identified link. They are usually underlined and shown in a different color.
● Move the mouse cursor over the underlined text.
● If the cursor changes to a hand, the text is "hot."
● Click the mouse button once to follow that link.

VISITED LINKS

As you follow hypertext links within a single website you may start to notice two colors of links on the web pages. This is because the links you have visited usually change color as a way of helping you keep track of where you have and have not been.

USING A NEW WINDOW

When you are browsing the web, it can be useful to open a page in a new window so that you have two or more browser windows open at the same time. You can continue to explore one page while another is being downloaded. To open any link in a new window, place the mouse cursor over the link, right-click the mouse and choose **Open Link in New Window** from the pop-up menu that appears.

RECOGNIZING NAVIGATION BUTTONS

Many websites use graphically styled buttons as the main way of navigating around the site. These buttons often appear at the top, bottom, or side of a page.

● Move the mouse cursor over some of the different buttons.

● Wherever the cursor changes to a hand there is a link from that image.

● Click the mouse button once when you want to follow a particular link.

Navigation buttons

RECOGNIZING IMAGE LINKS

Some of the more design-conscious websites use image "maps" to provide links. These appear on the page as a single image, different parts of which link to different places. As many of these images have no text labels to act as signposts, they offer a more exploratory and intuitive kind of surfing. Again, the way to discover such links is to move the mouse cursor over the images and see if it changes to a hand.

NAVIGATING BACK AND FORTH

Following links is simple once you know how, but before long you may find that you have completely moved away from where you started, and are not sure how to get back. You may also have encountered a few interesting pages on the way but failed to note their addresses. How do you return to find them again? Internet Explorer provides several features that enable you to move between the pages you have visited. Open any web page and follow between six and ten different links, then practice navigating using some of the techniques described below.

BACKWARD AND FORWARD PAGE BY PAGE

● Moving back is the most common operation you'll perform. To move back to the previous page you visited, place the cursor over the **Back** button on the toolbar and click once. Repeat the process to move back through several pages.
● To move forward to the page you were on before

you pressed **Back**, place the cursor over the **Forward** button and click once.

Repeat the process to move forward to the most recent page you opened.

BACK USING THE MENU

● To move back to any page you have visited in the current session, position the mouse cursor over the arrow to the right of the **Back** button and click once. Select the page you wish to return to from the drop-down menu that appears.

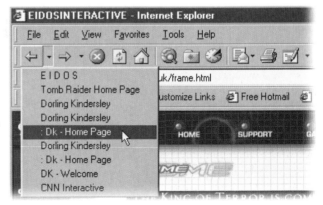

FORWARD USING THE MENU

- To move forward to any page that you accessed in the current session before you used the **Back** feature, position the mouse pointer over the arrow to the right of the **Forward** button and click once.
- Select the page you wish to return to from the drop-down menu that appears.

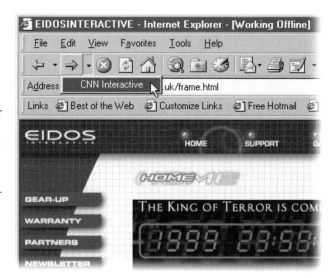

USING THE ADDRESS MENU

Explorer makes its own list of sites you visit regularly or access specifically by typing the address. You can access any of the sites on this list by positioning the mouse over the arrow at the end of the address bar and clicking once. A drop-down menu will appear. Use the scroll bar to see the full list. Position the mouse cursor over the address of interest and click once to promote that address into the address bar. If a connection is not made automatically, click **Go** or press the [Enter↵] key to make the connection.

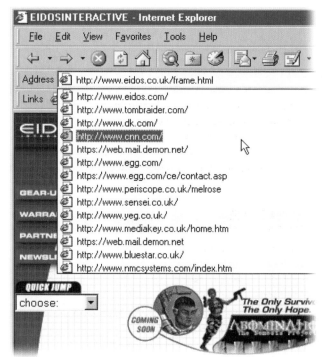

USING THE GO TO MENU

The **Go To** menu provides a list of all the sites you have visited in the current session, regardless of whether they came before or after the page you are currently on. To access this menu, click on **View** in the menu bar and select **Go To**. The list of sites appears in the lowest section of the drop-down submenu. Position the mouse cursor over the site you wish to access and click once.

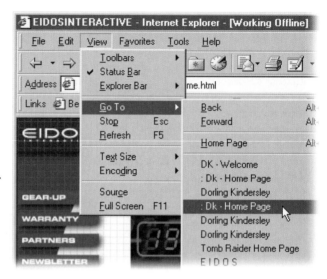

USING THE BROWSING HISTORY

Another means of accessing websites that you have already visited is to use Internet Explorer's History feature. This maintains a record of all the websites that you have visited during the current session as well as over the last few days or weeks. You can specify how many days you would like

Explorer to keep items in its History, and you can also clear all items from this memory whenever you wish to start afresh. Once you have visited a few websites, open the **History** panel and try returning to a site you visited earlier by following these instructions.

OPENING THE HISTORY PANEL

● To see a list of all the items stored in History, position the mouse cursor over the **History** button on the main toolbar and click once. The **History** panel will open inside the Explorer window.

OPEN A PAGE
IN THE LIST

● Position the mouse cursor over any page in the list so that it turns into a hand. A drop-down list appears showing the pages in that site you have visited. Click once to open the page you want in the main browser window.

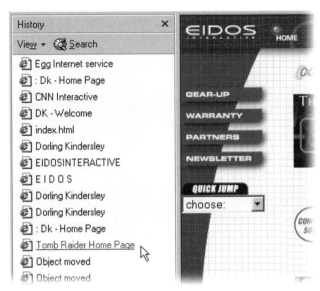

Sorting the History

You can sort the History pages by clicking the small arrow to the right of the **View** button in the **History** bar. A drop-down menu appears from which you can select to sort by date, site, the most visited, or in the order the pages have been visited today.

CHANGING THE
LENGTH OF TIME
SITES REMAIN IN
HISTORY

● Click on the **Tools** menu, select **Internet Options**, and the **Internet Options** dialog box opens showing the **General** settings.

● At the bottom of this page is the **History** subsection. To change the number of days for which History will remember sites, position the mouse cursor in the box to the right of **Days to keep pages in history**, and double-click to select the number in the box. When it is highlighted, type the required number of days. Click on the **OK** button at the foot of the dialog box.

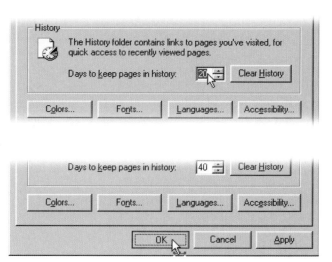

CLEARING THE HISTORY

● Open the **Internet Options** dialog box as described opposite. Position the mouse cursor over the **Clear History** button in the History panel and then click the **OK** button to close the box.

CLOSING THE HISTORY PANEL

● Position the mouse cursor over the X on the **History** bar and click once.

FAVORITES

Internet Explorer provides a way for you to create a digital bookmark for any site as a "favorite," which adds it to a special list that you can access quickly and easily whenever you wish.

THE FAVORITES PANEL

One of the features of Internet Explorer is a window that you can have open all the time on the left-hand side of the main browser window. It is called the Favorites panel, and from this panel you can access and organize your collection of favorites.

Explorer provides some suggested favorite places to get you started. Once you have connected to the internet, you can try accessing some favorites using the **Favorites** panel and some of the other methods described in this chapter.

OPENING THE FAVORITES PANEL

● Position the mouse cursor over the **Favorites** button on the main toolbar and click once.
● The **Favorites** panel will open on screen in the left-hand side of the main Explorer window.

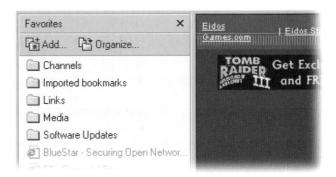

OPENING A FAVORITE SITE

● In the **Favorites** panel, position the mouse cursor over the site that you wish to open. When the cursor turns into a hand, click once to open that site in the main window.

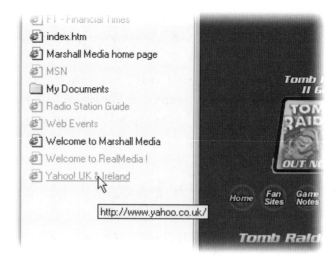

CLOSING THE FAVORITES PANEL

● When you have finished using your favorites, you can close the **Favorites** panel by positioning the mouse cursor over the X in the **Favorites** bar and clicking once. The main browser window expands to fill the available space.

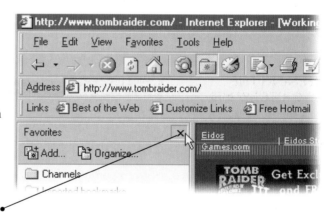

Close button ●

OPENING A FAVORITE USING THE FAVORITES MENU

You can also access your favorites directly from the **Favorites** menu. The advantage of using the menu instead of the panel is that you have a larger window area in which to view the web pages you select. To open a favorite using this method, position the mouse cursor over the **Favorites** menu and click once. A drop-down menu will appear, listing all your current favorites. Move the mouse cursor over the one of interest (submenus appear next to folders). When it becomes highlighted, click the mouse once to open it.

CREATING YOUR OWN FAVORITES

As your experience of finding your way around the World Wide Web increases, it is inevitable that you will accumulate a selection of sites that you refer to more than any others: your preferred search engine 🗋, news providers, your bank, particular companies, and sites offering a little light relief, for example. These sites are the perfect candidates to be your favorite places. Adding one of these sites to your favorites is very simple and can be done by using the **Favorites** panel or via the **Favorites** menu, depending on how you prefer to use your browser. Connect to the internet and open a site that you would like to add to your favorite places. Then follow the instructions below, using whichever method you prefer.

1 CREATING USING FAVORITES PANEL

● Position the mouse cursor over the **Favorites** button on the main toolbar and click once to display the **Favorites** panel on screen.
● In the **Favorites** panel, position the mouse cursor over the **Add** button and click once. Now go to Step 3.

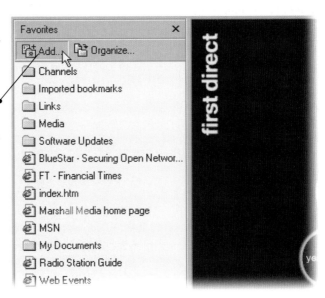

Add button •

Keyboard favorites
Once you are familiar with creating your own favorites, you'll feel confident about using the keyboard shortcut to creating a favorite, which is to hold down the Ctrl key and press D.

Using Search Engines

128

2 CREATING USING FAVORITES MENU

● Alternatively, position the mouse cursor over **Favorites** on the menu bar and click once to activate the **Favorites** menu. Position the mouse cursor over **Add to Favorites** and click once when it becomes highlighted.

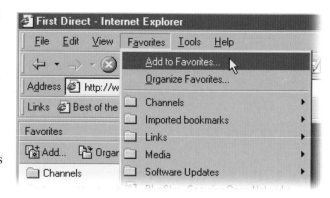

3 NAMING A FAVORITE

● Whichever method you use, the **Add Favorite** dialog box will now open and the name of the favorite you have just created will be shown in the **Name** box. If you would like to change the name, position the mouse cursor after the text in the **Name** box and click once. A flashing insertion point will appear. Press the [← Bksp] key and hold it down until all the text has been deleted.

● Now type your preferred name for this favorite. If you wish to store the favorite in a particular folder go to Step 4, otherwise click on **OK**.

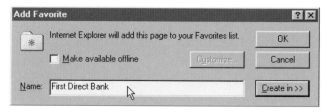

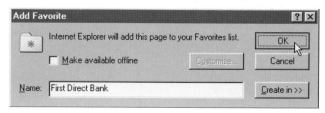

4 FILING A FAVORITE

● In the **Add Favorite** box, click the **Create in** button to open the Favorites directory. Navigate to the folder you wish to store the favorite in. Double-click on the folder to open it and single-click on a folder to select it.

● When you have selected the folder, position the mouse cursor over the **OK** button at the top and click once to save the favorite in the chosen folder.

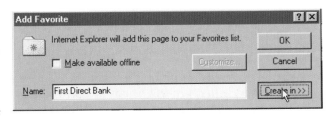

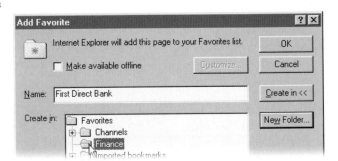

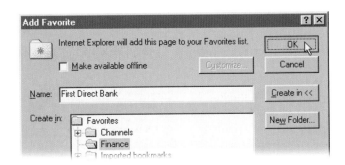

MAKING FAVORITES AVAILABLE OFFLINE

If you access some of your favorite places frequently, you can make them available for offline browsing. This means that the page will be saved locally on your computer and you will not need to connect to your service provider every time you want to see it. This will save your phone bills, but it will also mean that if the site is updated often you may not have the latest information. To make a page available for viewing offline, position the mouse cursor over the favorite and right-click. Place the mouse cursor over Choose Make Available Offline from the pop-up menu and left-click.

ORGANIZING YOUR FAVORITES

You will find that your list of favorites grows very quickly, and you may find it helpful to create a structured filing system for them so that you can easily find the things you are looking for. You can do this with folders in much the same way that you organize any other files that you store on your computer. Because the web is changing all the time, you may also find occasions when you go to a favorite only to discover that it no longer exists. It is easy to delete an obsolete favorite from the list. All these functions can be managed from the **Organize Favorites** box. This box can be accessed from the **Favorites** panel or from the **Favorites** menu.

1 ORGANIZING IN FAVORITES PANEL

● Position the mouse cursor over the **Favorites** button on the main toolbar and click once.

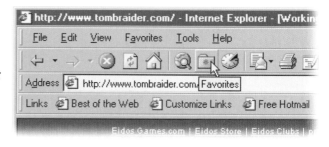

● Position the mouse cursor over the **Organize** button in the **Favorites** panel and click once.

● The **Organize Favorites** box will open.

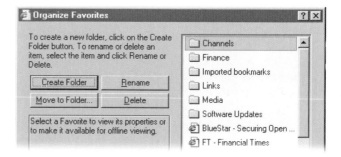

2 ORGANIZING IN FAVORITES MENU

● Alternatively, position the mouse cursor over **Favorites** on the menu bar and click once.

● Position the mouse cursor over **Organize Favorites** and click once.

● The **Organize Favorites** box will open.

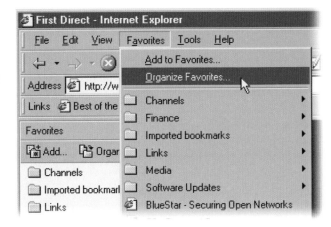

CREATING A NEW FOLDER

● To create a new folder on the top level simply click the **Create Folder** button. A new folder will appear in the list on the right.

● Type the name of the folder and then press the [Enter ←] key.

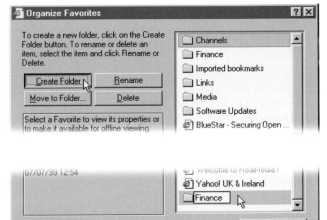

● To create a folder within another folder, first click on the folder in the list on the right so that it becomes highlighted.

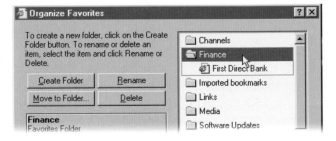

● Now click the **Create Folder** button. Then type the name as in step 2.

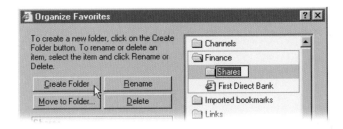

MOVING A FAVORITE

● To move a favorite from one folder to another, click on the favorite in the list on the right so that it is highlighted.

● Click the **Move to Folder** button. The **Browse for Folder** window will open.

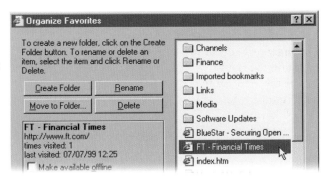

Drag and drop

If you can see the location to which you want to move a favorite, you can place the cursor over it, hold down the mouse button and "drag" it to the new location where it can be "dropped."

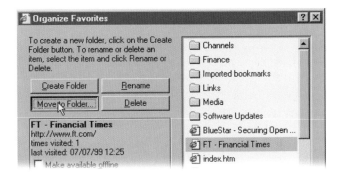

● In the **Browse for Folder** window, navigate to the folder you wish to store the favorite in, double-click on a folder to open it and single-click on a folder to select it.

● When you have selected the folder, position the mouse cursor over the **OK** button and click once to move the favorite to the chosen folder.

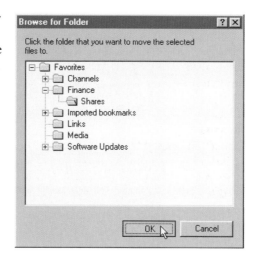

DELETING A FAVORITE

● To delete a favorite, click on the favorite in the list on the right so that it is highlighted.

● Position the mouse cursor over the **Delete** button and click once.

● Click **Yes** in the **Confirm File Delete** box to delete the favorite. The favorite will disappear from the list.

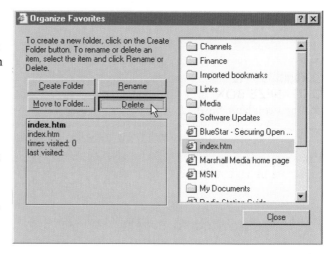

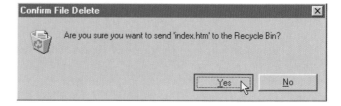

RENAMING A FAVORITE

● To rename a favorite, click on the favorite in the list on the right so that it is highlighted.
● Position the mouse cursor over the **Rename** button and click once. The name of the favorite will become highlighted in a box that you can edit.
● Type in the new name and press the [Enter ←] key when you have finished. You will see the name change in the list.

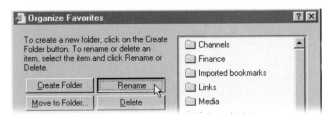

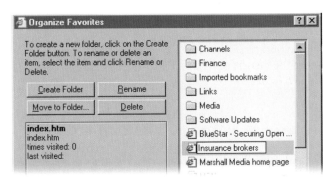

CLOSING THE ORGANIZE BOX

● When you have finished, close the **Organize Favorites** box by positioning the mouse cursor over the **Close** button and clicking.

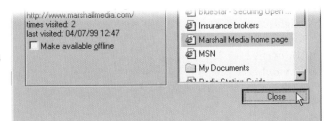

USING THE RIGHT MOUSE BUTTON

With the **Favorites** panel open in the browser window, you can perform several of the activities shown here, such as deleting and renaming, directly from the panel by using the right mouse button. Position the mouse cursor over any favorite and click the right mouse button once. You will see a pop-up menu with **Delete** and **Rename** as options. Move the mouse cursor over the desired option and click the left mouse button to activate it. If you choose **Delete**, you will be asked to confirm the action. Click **Yes** to proceed. If you select **Rename**, a text box that you can edit will appear. Type the new name and press the [Enter ←] key when you have finished.

PERSONALIZING

Internet Explorer is configured using Microsoft's default settings. However, it is possible to personalize the way Internet Explorer looks and works to suit your own preferences.

THE INTERNET OPTIONS WINDOW

The Internet Options window is where you can change Explorer's default settings. It allows you to change aspects such as display settings, security features, connection details, content control, storage of internet files by the cache, and other features. Most settings referred to in this chapter can be changed using the Internet Options window, which can be opened from within Internet Explorer, or from the desktop (when the same window will be called Internet Properties).

OPENING INTERNET OPTIONS WINDOW FROM THE MENU

● With Internet Explorer open, position the mouse cursor over **Tools** on the main menu and click once to open the **Tools** menu. Highlight **Internet Options** on the menu and click once to open the **Internet Options** window.

OPENING FROM THE DESKTOP

● Alternatively position the mouse cursor over the Explorer icon on the desktop. Click the right mouse button, highlight **Properties** in the pop-up menu that appears, and click the left mouse button to open the **Internet Properties** window.

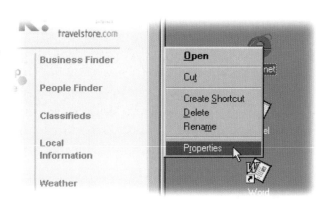

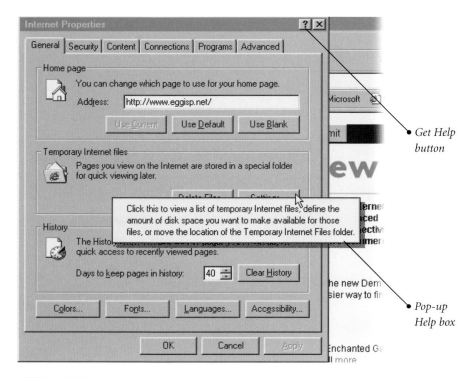

Get Help button

Pop-up Help box

HELP WITH INTERNET OPTIONS

● If you are not sure what an Internet Option does, you can get help by clicking on the question mark at top right of the Internet Options window. A question mark is attached to the cursor, which you can then move to the option you need help with and clicking once. A Help box pops up telling you about that option.

SAVING YOUR OPTIONS

● When you have made any changes to the Internet Options, click on the **OK** button to save the changes. Click **Cancel** if you do not want to save the changes.

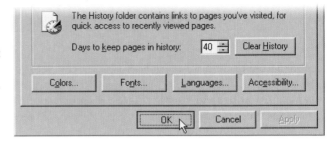

CHANGING THE DISPLAY SETTINGS

Web designers often specify the color, size and font for text, the color of links, and background color as part of an integral design of their sites. If you cannot read the text easily, you can override the default settings of the page. The downside is that the look of web pages may be adversely affected. Text may not flow neatly around images, and some images may appear transparent or fuzzy when viewed against a background color they were not designed for. However, you can choose to use your preferred settings all the time, or only when a design has not been specified.

CHANGING FONT SIZE FROM THE MENU

You can increase or decrease the size of the text used on web pages.

● Click on **View** in the menu bar and highlight **Text Size**. A submenu appears.

● Move the cursor over your preferred option and click with the left mouse button.

● The setting you choose will remain in force until you change it again.

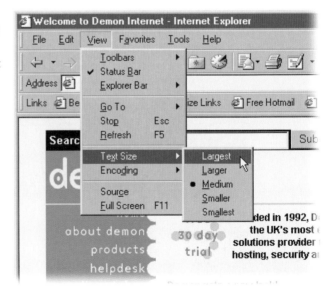

CHOOSING THE TYPEFACE

Under the **General** tab of **Internet Options** you can choose which font, or typeface, you would like Internet Explorer to use. The font you choose will be used when a typeface has not been specified in a web page as part of its design. To choose a font, first open the **Internet Options** window 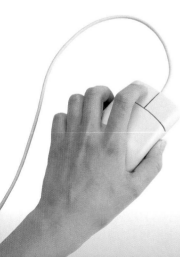, place the cursor over the **General** tab, click once to bring it to the front, and follow these instructions.

● Click the **Fonts** button at the foot of the window to open the **Fonts** box.

● In the **Fonts** dialog box use the scroll bars to find your preferred font, place the cursor over it and click to highlight it, then click the **OK** button to select it and return to Internet Options.

● Save your options 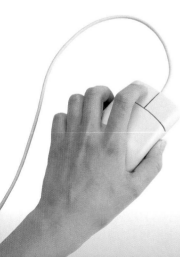 to apply the new settings.

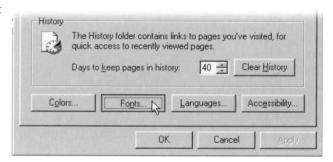

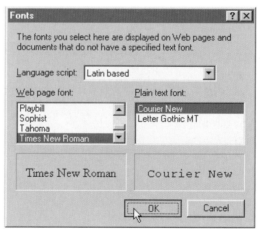

92 The Internet Options Window

94 Saving your options

CHOOSING HYPERLINK COLORS

You can specify the colors that display normal text, and for unvisited and visited hyperlinks ⬜. You can also choose a "hover" color. If you choose a hover color, a hyperlink changes to that color when you roll the cursor over that link.

SETTING A COLOR

● Whether you want to set a text, hyperlink, or a background color, begin by opening the Internet Options window ⬜, and click on the **General** tab to bring it to the front if it is not already displayed.

● Click the **Colors** button at the foot of the window to open the **Colors** dialog box.

● In the **Colors** dialog box click the mouse in the **Use Windows colors** check box to remove the check mark if there is one in the box.

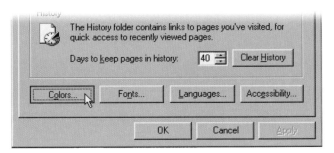

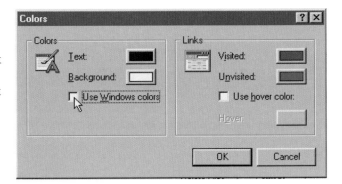

● Click the color box next to either **Text** or **Background**, depending on which of the two settings you want to change.

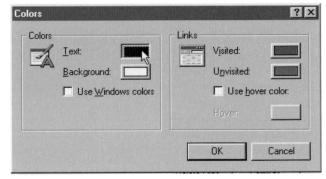

75 **Recognizing hypertext links**

92 **The Internet Options Window**

● Click on your preferred color in the color palette, then click on **OK**. When you want to return to the default text color, simply put a check mark back in the **Use Windows colors** check box.

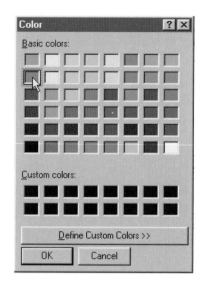

● Change the visited and unvisited hyperlink colors by following the same process in the **Links** panel.

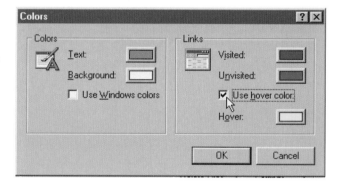

● To set a hover color, click the mouse in the **Use hover color** check box and then click on the color button next to Hover. Select your preferred color from the color palette as before.
● Click on the **OK** button at the bottom to leave the **Colors** dialog box, then save your options to apply the changes.

OVERRIDING PAGE DISPLAY SETTINGS

The font and color settings that you choose are only used if a web page does not specify these options in its design, but with web developers becoming ever more design conscious, most now tend to specify fonts, font sizes, and colors. If you would prefer to use your settings all the time when using the web, you can elect to override the design style of the page using Explorer's **Accessibility** options. These **Accessibility** options are found under the **General** tab of the **Internet Options**. You can choose to override web page font, background color, and font point size settings, or only a selection of these features. First, open the **Internet Options** window ⌐ and click the mouse over the **General** tab to bring it to the front.

● Click the **Accessibility** button at the bottom of the window to open the **Accessibility** dialog box.

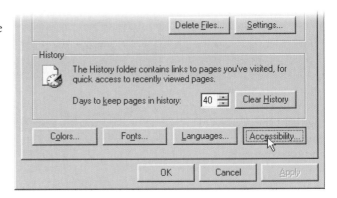

● Place the cursor over the check box next to the option you want to set and click to place a check mark in the box. Then click on **OK** to close the **Accessibility** box.
● Save your options ⌐ to apply the changes.

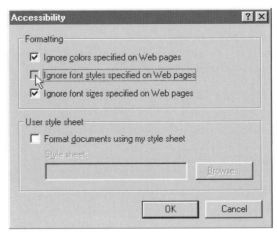

92 The Internet Options Window

94 Saving your Options

CHANGING YOUR HOME PAGE

The home page is the page that opens each time you start Internet Explorer. When you first install Explorer, the home page is usually configured to open Microsoft's website. There may well be information of interest to you on Microsoft's site, but it is more likely to be of only occasional interest. The ideal home page would be a page that you will want to open each time you connect. It might be a useful jumping off point or source of information you require regularly. The page you choose will depend mainly on how you use the web. Among the possible contenders as your home page might be your favorite search engine, news site, share tracker, bookstore, game site, chat site, your Internet Service Provider, or email access on the web. Changing the home page is simple and can be done from the **General** tab in the **Internet Options** window.

● In the **Home Page** section of the **Internet Options** dialog box, double-click the mouse in the **Address** field to highlight the address of your current home page, and type the address of your new home page.

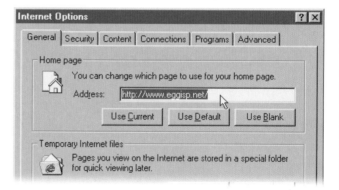

● You can click **Use Current** if you want to use the web page that is currently displayed behind the **Internet Options** dialog box as your home page.

● Save your options to apply the changes. This page now appears when you start Internet Explorer or when you click the **Home** button on the toolbar.

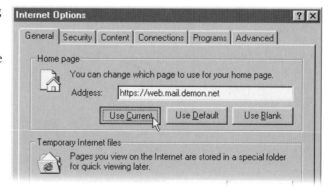

Managing the Cache

The cache is an area of temporary memory on your hard disk where Explorer stores temporary internet files. These are transferred to your computer when you request a web page. They display the web page and include the image, text, and multimedia files. Explorer stores these files so that time can be saved by loading the page from the hard disk if you revisit the page. You may want to clear the cache to save space, you may want to open a page from the cache, or tell Explorer how often to compare a cached page to one on the web. These instructions show you how.

CLEARING THE CACHE

● You access the cache by first opening the **Internet Options** window and clicking the **General** tab.

● Position the mouse over the **Delete Files** button in the **Temporary Internet files** section to clear the cache of these temporary internet files.

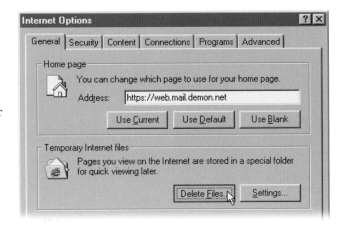

OPENING THE CACHE SETTINGS

● Position the cursor over the **Settings** button to open the **Settings** dialog box, and click once.

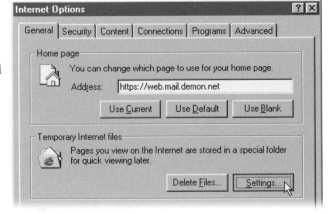

The dialog box options determine how often Explorer checks the cache.

● Choose **Every visit to the page** if you want to make sure you always have the most recent version of a web page.

● Click the **View Files** button to see a list of files stored in the cache. You can open any of these files in Explorer by double-clicking them with the mouse.

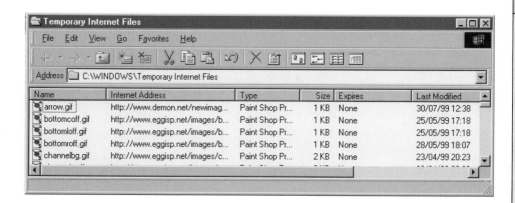

● Click **OK** to leave the **Settings** box. Save your options to apply the changes you have made.

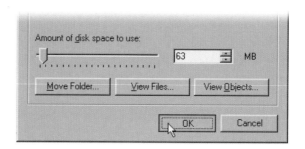

Saving your options

HANDLING MULTIMEDIA FILES

If you are using the internet with a slow modem connection, you may decide not to download images and other multimedia files because they slow down the speed at which a web page is downloaded to your computer. Explorer lets you specify which types of files to turn off in the **Advanced** section of **Internet Options**.

● Open the **Internet Options** window ⬚ and click on the **Advanced** tab to bring it to the front.
● Use the scroll bar to scroll down until the **Multimedia** icon is at the top of the window.
● If you want to disable any multimedia files, and they are already checked, click the mouse in the check box next to the relevant options from **Play animations**, **Play Sounds**, **Play videos**, and **Show pictures**.
● Save your options ⬚ to apply the changes.

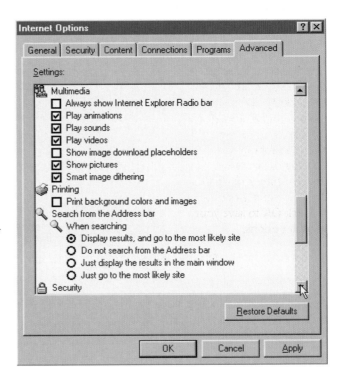

MULTIMEDIA PLUG-INS

Internet Explorer 5 comes with three multimedia "plug-in" programs pre-installed: Shockwave, Flash, and RealPlayer. These plug-ins enable you to view most of the animations, sound files, and videos used on the internet. If a web page requires a different plug-in, you will be prompted to install it. This is usually just a process of downloading the software and installing it, then returning to the web page to see what it has to offer.

| 92 | **The Internet Options Window** | | 94 | **Saving your options** |

CHOOSING PROGRAMS

Explorer provides its own email and newsreading facilities, in the shape of the Outlook Express program, but if you already have email or newsreading programs installed on your computer, your can opt to use those programs instead of Outlook Express. By setting your program preferences, you are able to access your other programs directly when you choose email or News from Explorer's Tools menu. Follow these instructions to set up the available program options. First, open the **Internet Options** dialog box ⌐ and click the **Programs** tab.

● Choose your preferred option for each of these program types by clicking the arrows to view a list of programs to choose from. Select a program by moving the mouse, highlighting, and clicking on the desired program.
● Click **OK** to save your chosen options.

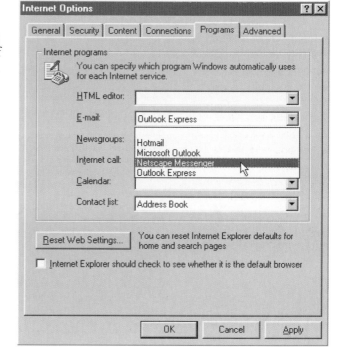

SETTING UP SECURITY

With the global expansion of electronic commerce, and money changing hands over the internet around the clock, online security is an important issue, but one that can only be touched on here. Internet Explorer provides several types of security settings. It allows you to set the level of risk that you are prepared to take when receiving data over the internet. For example, how likely is the data to harm your computer with a virus? It also offers control over the type of content you receive; and it has features that enable you to identify secure and trusted websites. This is particularly important since the advent of online shopping.

SETTING THE ZONE AND LEVEL

The Internet Options **Security** tab enables you to categorize particular websites into various zones, such as trusted or restricted, and set the level of security you would like to operate across each zone, such as high or low security risk. You may want to set up this security for "secure" websites where you can shop or send confidential information. To set up the security for a zone, follow this sequence:

● Position the mouse cursor over the relevant icon in the top panel and click to highlight it.

● Click on the **Sites** button to add a site to that zone (this option is only available for the Trusted and Restricted zones).

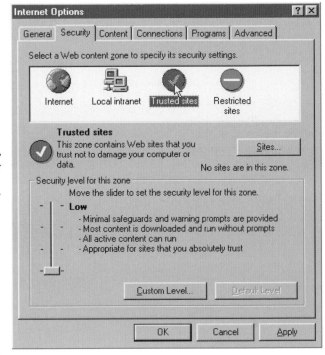

● The **Trusted sites** dialog box opens. Type the address of the website you would like to add in the **Add this Web site to the zone** field, then click **OK**.

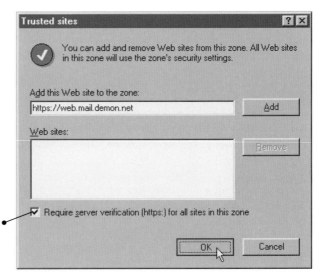

Check this box if you want this zone to include "secure" websites, that are prefixed by https:// only.

● Use the mouse to drag the **Security level** slider to the desired position (you will see the name of the level change as you move the slider).
● Click **OK** to save your changes or repeat the sequence for another zone.

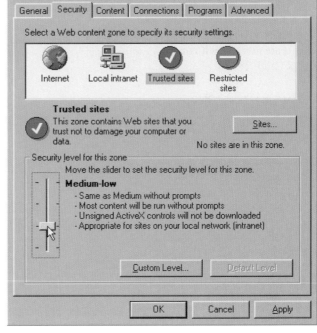

CONTROLLING CONTENT

As well as being the home to millions of interesting sites, the web is also fertile ground for pornography and many other forms of unauthorized, offensive, and illegal information. To prevent your web browser from being used to view sites that contain this kind of material, you can use Explorer's **Content Advisor** features. These enable you to censor sites that feature bad language, nudity, sex, and violence.

● First, open the **Internet Options** window ⌂ and click the **Content** tab.
● In the **Content Advisor** dialog box, click on the **Enable** button.

● On the **Ratings** tab, click on and highlight the type of content that you want to control in the **Select a category** window.

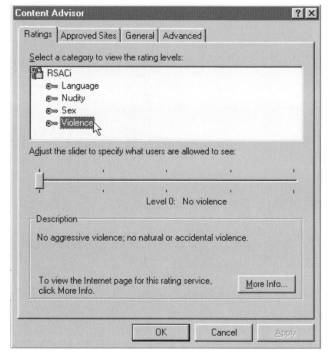

● Drag the slider across to the desired level of access (you will see information about the levels as you move the slider).

● Repeat this process for each of the content types you want to control.

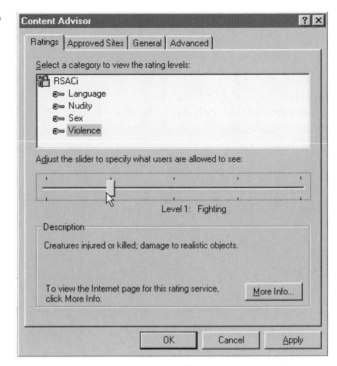

● Click the **OK** button.

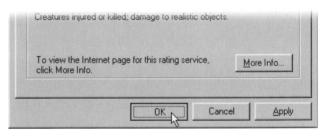

● Type your password in both fields of the **Create Supervisor Password** box. (Remember to make a note of this somewhere safe!) Now click on **OK**.

● Your content security is now set up and only you, as the holder of the password, can alter the settings.

SEARCHING THE INTERNET

S EARCHING THE INTERNET is an easy-to-follow guide to using your PC to explore the internet. You will find explanations on everything from understanding the toolbars to choosing a search provider. This section will help you to get the most out of searching the internet. It takes you through simple and advanced searching; explains how to use different search commands; and gives you an overview of the major search engines and directories, as well as telling you the differences between the two. It also provides you with details about specialized search providers that can help you to find people, news, and software.

WINDOW ON THE WEB

The web browser program installed on your PC is the window through which you view the web. As well as taking you straight to known web addresses, it is the starting point for any search.

SEARCHING EFFICIENTLY

For millions of people around the world, the internet has become an invaluable treasure house of information, a vast source of software, music, games, pictures, and data. Over the last year or so, it has also become a global online shopping mall. Whatever you're looking for, it's probably available via the net.

SAVING VALUABLE TIME

Surprisingly, very few people think about how to make their internet searching as efficient as possible. As a newcomer to the internet, you may enjoy "surfing" through endless websites in the course of your quest but, as you may already have discovered, a search in its simplest form can return many thousands of suggested websites that would take hours to sift through. As the novelty wears off and the internet becomes an increasingly essential tool, rather than a new toy, this book will help you to search quickly and efficiently. By following the step-by-step instructions and learning how a variety of search tools work, you will soon be able to:

1 choose the right search tool for the job
2 structure your search queries efficiently
3 become a power user of search tools.

Order out of chaos
The internet has been described as the new Wild West and, because of its nature, imposing any order is almost impossible. You can, however, impose your own order on this chaos by knowing how to search it.

STARTING FROM THE BROWSER

A web browser is a piece of software installed on your PC that lets you look at (or "browse") different websites. It also enables you to start a search, and will connect you to the search engines that can help you find what you're looking for. The most widely used web browsers are Netscape Navigator and Microsoft Internet Explorer. In the examples shown in this book, we have used Internet Explorer, but they are both excellent browsers. You can have both of them installed on your PC at the same time, and which one you use is a matter of personal preference.

WHAT IS EXPLORER?

Microsoft Internet Explorer comes as a standard part of Windows software and was probably already installed on your computer when it arrived. A suite of internet-related programs that includes Outlook Express and FrontPage, Internet Explorer enables you to connect to websites and view them, surf the web using hypertext links, and download programs and files from the internet

Seen Through Explorer
For full details of this program works, the Browsing the Web *section in this* Essential Internet Guide $\Box$.

to your own computer. By default, its email features operate through Outlook Express, and its Edit feature is directly linked to FrontPage, which can be used to create and publish your own web pages.

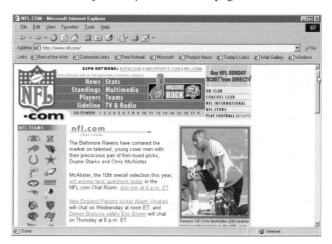

DIFFERENCES IN APPEARANCE

Most websites look the same whatever browser you use. But you might notice small changes if you view the same page using different browsers. This is because the language used for web pages (called Hypertext Markup Language, or HTML) describes how a page appears, and different browsers may interpret the HTML instructions differently.

THE EXPLORER TOOLBARS

It is perfectly possible to use Internet Explorer using only the features provided on the standard buttons toolbar. This toolbar is at the top of the Explorer window and comprises a row of graphically styled buttons. These buttons are shortcuts to features that will help you find your way round the web quickly, so it is worth spending time familiarizing yourself with the toolbar and learning what each symbol means. Each item on the toolbar is also in the main menus.

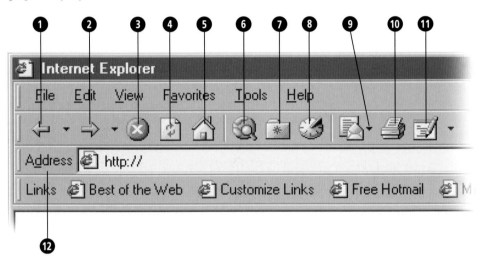

THE STANDARD TOOLBAR

❶ Back
❷ Forward
These two buttons take you backward and forward through the web pages you have already visited.
❸ Stop
Stops a page downloading.
❹ Refresh
Refreshes the current page.
❺ Home
Loads the default home page.

❻ Search
Opens the Search panel in the Explorer window. This gives you access to features that help you connect to search engines.
❼ Favorites
Opens the Favorites panel, which allows you to create, access, and manage your favorite sites on the web.
❽ History
Opens the History panel.

❾ Mail
Provides a menu of options related to email.
❿ Print
Prints the current page.
⓫ Edit
Allows you to edit the code of the current web page.
⓬ Address bar
Allows you to type in the address of a known website and go directly to that site.

RUNNING A SIMPLE SEARCH

In the very simplest form of search carried out using Internet Explorer, the search term is typed in, and a designated search engine returns a list of sites. The problem is that there may be thousands of sites with varying degrees of relevance.

1 CHOOSING THE SEARCH BUTTON
● With Internet Explorer running, click the **Search** button on the toolbar. This will create a frame on the left of the browser window.

2 KEYING IN THE SEARCH TERM
● Type a search term in the search text box and click on **Search.** The search begins.
● Note that there is a **Customize** button in this frame. Clicking on this allows you to choose the categories of search and which search engines you wish to use. In this case the search engine is Excite.

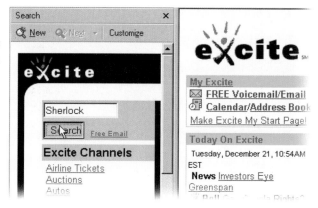

3 LIST OF HITS
● When the list of hits appears in the left-hand frame, hold the mouse pointer over any entry to see the address and a brief description of the website. Click any entry to display that site in the main part of the browser window.

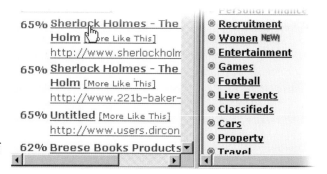

4 USING THE ADDRESS BAR

● You can also run a search on the internet directly from the Internet Explorer Address bar by typing **go**, **find**, or **?** followed by the search term.

● After typing your search query, press the [Enter ⏎] key. The left-hand "search" panel of the browser window will open, if it is not open already, and the search will start.

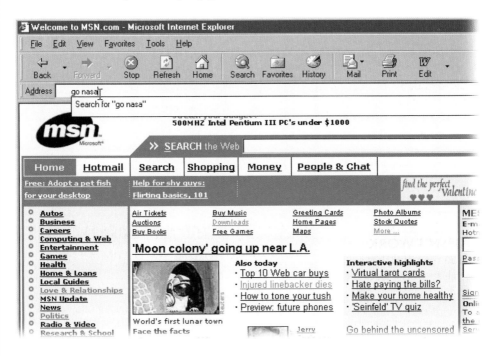

SEARCHING FROM THE DESKTOP

You can access the internet search tool for your browser at any time by clicking the **Start** button, then choosing **On the Internet** from the drop down **Find** menu. This will launch Internet Explorer if you are not already using it.

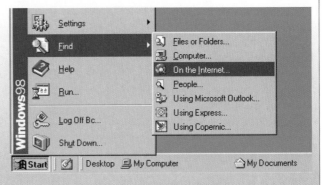

● When searching from the **Address** bar, Internet Explorer will automatically display the web page that matches your search term most closely, as well as showing a list of hits.

● You may be lucky and find just the site you want, but this can be a very hit or miss method if your search term is very broad.

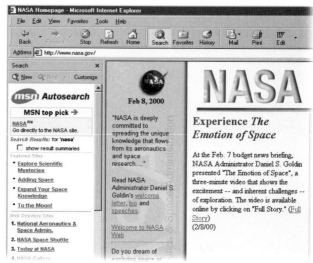

IF THIS METHOD DOESN'T WORK

● You may find that a search from the **Address** bar fails to work in this way. If so, check that the options are correctly set.

● From the **Tools** menu at the top of your screen, select **Internet Options** (indicated by a magnifying glass icon) and then click on the **Advanced** tab to bring this page to the front. Scroll down to **Search from the Address bar,** and click on the **Display results, and go to the most likely site** radio button if it is not already selected. Then click on **OK**.

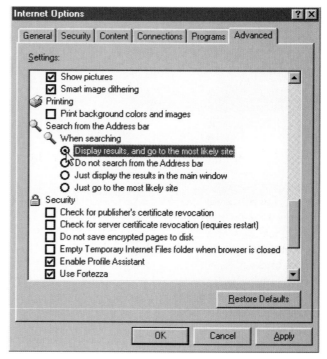

92 **The Internet Options Window**

SEARCH TOOLS

Web searching is made possible through the services of search providers, who offer software and databases that are accessed through the web browser or through the provider's website.

WHAT DO SEARCH TOOLS DO?

When you use a search engine, web directory, or internet search program of any kind, you are never running a "live" search of what is on the internet at that moment. You are really using a program to interrogate a database owned by the search provider, and which may contain information from millions of pages.

DIFFERENT WAYS OF WORKING

Despite the similarity between the "portal" interfaces of the most visited search tools, you will soon find that search providers return widely differing search results and present them in different ways. This is because the databases on which these engines and directories are based are built and managed in very different ways. The first reason for this is the differing information on the search providers' databases. This information has to be collected, collated, and organized before it is ready for public

Accessing information
The way in which data is collected, stored, and organized in a database will affect the quality of the results it provides.

use, and every search provider carries out these stages in a different way. Some databases are more current than others, or are larger and contain more data. Some search providers can deliver results more quickly than others, and some have more user-friendly or more easily customized interfaces. Some providers are selective in what they collect and may provide site reviews. Others process all the data on a web page regardless of its content or quality, and although the database may therefore look as though it is more comprehensive, it may actually be less efficient and offer less useful search results.

DIFFERENT RESULTS

These differences explain why the same search query can produce very different outcomes. Search results from different providers vary in terms of:

- speed of response
- total number of hits
- number of relevant hits
- position of relevant hits
- presentation of hits.

The factors that tend to make us favor one search provider over another relate to the efficiency and usability of the interface. In the end, your choice will usually be determined partly from personal preference for the interface and partly because you want to pick the right tool for a particular type of search. However, there are other important considerations.

DIRECTORIES AND ENGINES

One important element that distinguishes one search provider from another is the way they make the information stored in their databases available. Yahoo and Lycos are directory-based , classifying the data like a table of contents, whereas AltaVista and Excite are search engines  that rely heavily on their powerful search software.

WEB DIRECTORY OR SEARCH ENGINE?

A web directory is essentially a list of links, usually accompanied by a site description and sometimes a review. The user starts at a top level category, or classification, and then drills down through a series of subcategories until reaching the specific subject area and the required website.

A search engine enables a user to search a database created by the search provider. A search engine provides pages of hits – often thousands of them – arranged by relevance to the query. In either case, the speed with which a particular search tool produces the results you need and the ease with which you can use its tools and access the results are key factors in determining whether or not you use it for your search.

Speed of search
How long does it take to give useful results?

Ease of use
Only using a search tool will show you how easy it is to access its features and the search results.

|118| **Web Directories**

|123| **Search Engines**

WEB DIRECTORIES

Web page author submits URL to the web directory

Web site owners submit their site's address, or URL (standing for "Uniform Resource Locator"), to the search engine 📄. Most search engines and web directories provide a "Submit your Site" option on their main web page to allow the authors of web pages to do this. A reviewer then assesses the page and decides whether to include it in the directory. This process can take several weeks, or even months for some directories.

Web directory reviewer/editor assesses the submission

Search Provider's database
If the web reviewer passes the page for inclusion, it will be categorized before being placed in the web directory

Some web pages are rejected by the reviewer and do not make it into the directory

Searching the web
A description and URL for the web page will now appear in the appropriate category

How Does a Web Page Get There?

Information for web directories is compiled and collated (and often rejected) by reviewers and editors employed by search providers. Most providers offer a step-by-step method for submitting web pages for scrutiny, so this process can best be understood by looking at it from a web page author's point of view. For example, if you had just completed an illustrated history of backgammon, you might want to make it available through the search provider Yahoo! Using the web browser, you would first go to the Yahoo! home page and find the category in which the page should be placed by starting at one of the 14 top-level categories and drilling down to find the most appropriate subcategory for the page.

SUBMITTING THE WEB PAGE

For our backgammon example, this is fairly straightforward as there is a specific **Backgammon** subcategory within the **Recreation>Games>Board Games** section of the directory. Having located the appropriate page, all you need to do is click the **Suggest a Site** link at the foot of the screen. It is very important to follow this procedure carefully when registering a site with a search provider like Yahoo! because by giving the site reviewer the most useful information regarding the content and category of your site, you give it the best chance of inclusion in the directory. Directory users are very likely to do precisely what you have just done when looking for sites on backgammon. So your time and effort at this stage will be well-spent to make your site available to users.

- Backgammon Portal - offers concise, targeted backgammon links, rules and tips for beginner to advanced player more.
- British Isles Backgammon Association - offers a calendar of tournaments, results, rules of play, membership infor contacts, and more.
- Can A Fish Taste Twice as Good? - backgammon book; comprehensive study of doubling in an un-even match.
- Chicago Point Backgammon Online - an electronic preview of Chicago Point monthly backgammon newsletter; a source of backgammon information for thousands of players worldwide.
- gammon.com
- LadderFacts - provides Yahoo! Backgammon ladder players with info about the ladder, matches & players.
- Nevada Backgammon Association
- Usenet - rec.games.backgammon

Click Here for 101 Useful Websites.

http://add.yahoo.com/fast/add?147960   Internet

The first step in "posting" your site •

MAKING THE LINK

● After clicking **Suggest a link** in Yahoo! you are taken to a step-by-step sequence.

- You have read the brief explanation of how to suggest a site to Yahoo!
- You have searched the directory and confirmed that your site is not alr
- You have found an appropriate category for your site. (If you haven't explanation for help finding that category.)
- You have clicked on the "Suggest a Site" at the bottom of the page fro

If you answer "Yes" to all of the above, then please:

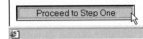

● In the online form that appears on screen, type some information about your web page following the bulleted advice below each box.

● This information helps the reviewer to decide whether you have chosen the correct category for your web page.

● The reviewer will then look at your web page and apply the search provider's acceptance criteria before deciding whether or not your page makes it into the directory's database.

Suggest a Site to Yahoo! - Step 1 - Microsoft Internet Explorer

File   Edit   View   Favorites   Tools   Help

Back   Forward   Stop   Refresh   Home   Search   Favorites   History   Mail

Address http://add.yahoo.com/fast/add

Site Information:

Title:
Backgammon through the ages

- Please keep the title brief.
- Use the official business name for the title of a commercial site.
- Please do not use ALL capital letters.
- Please do not including marketing slogans or superlatives (e.g., "The B the Number One Dealer...")

URL:
http://www.myisp.net/users/jsmith/home.htm

- Not sure what this is? It's the address of your site that begins with "http
- Please supply the entire URL and double check to make sure it is corr

Description:
Backgammon was played in ancient Mesopotamia, Greece, and

Always read the Help file...

Always read the Search provider's Help files before submitting a site. As well as helping web authors to promote their sites more efficiently, the Help files will also provide all users with useful information about how the search engine or web directory works. Reading these, in conjunction with the advanced search documentation, will quickly give you an understanding of the directory and make you a power user, which is never a bad thing!

CHANGING A WEB PAGE'S DIRECTORY LISTING

● If you add pages to a website that are likely to change its listing (for example, if your history of backgammon becomes a history of backgammon *and* checkers) you need to inform the directory provider. In the case of Yahoo! you would use the online **change form** option in the **Suggest a Site** page. Web directory reviewers need to be warned when a web page changes so that they can reassess the site and recategorize it.

● As you will see , search engines need no input from the web page author because they operate almost completely automatically. If you change your site, most search engines will pick up these changes and amend their databases.

How to Suggest a Change to Your Yahoo! Listing - Microsoft Internet Explorer

File   Edit   View   Favorites   Tools   Help

Back   Forward   Stop   Refresh   Home   Search   Favorites   History

Address   http://add.yahoo.com/fast/change

Please complete the following questions:

1. In order for us to make any modifications to your Yahoo! listing, we input the **exact** URL that Yahoo! provides for your site.

   Current URL:
   http://www.myisp.net/users/jsmith/home.htm

2. For security purposes, please tell us the email address of the contact It is the same email address you first gave us when you submitted the

   Current Email:
   jsmith@myisp.net

3. If you want to suggest a change to the title of your site, enter the *new* longer than five (5) words and not all capital letters (e.g. XYZ CORP INTERNET, etc.). For companies, the title MUST be the company something other than its actual name will be ignored.

   New Title:
   History of backgammon and checkers

Done

CONVERGING SERVICES

Yahoo! is, of course, only one of many web directories available free to users on the web. Many search engine providers now include a web directory on their websites, though on a far more modest scale than the Yahoo! directory. Many directory services now also offer a search engine. Rather than developing these additional services in-house, search providers are now commonly striking up partnership deals with each other, and it is not uncommon for several "rival" web directories to draw on the same database. However, the results are usually processed and presented in different ways, so that it is difficult for most of us to spot the shared connections.

SHARED DIRECTORIES

The directories featured here are evidence that databases are becoming more and more thorough in their coverage of the contents of the internet, and that these databases are being shared by an ever-growing number of search providers.

THE OPEN DIRECTORY PROJECT

This initiative aims to build a comprehensive directory of the web using mainly volunteer editors. In fact, at the ODP website (**dmoz.org**), you are encouraged to **Become an Editor.** You can choose a topic and, by using the tools provided, add, delete, and update links.

The Open Directory Project's data is used by a very large number of search providers including AltaVista, AOL Search, Dogpile, Lycos, Hotbot, and Netscape Search.

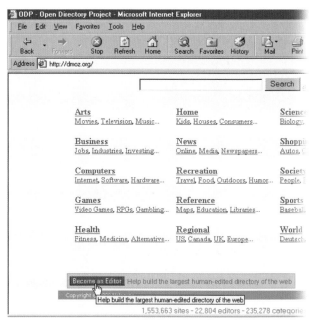

LEADING DIRECTORY PROVIDERS

One powerful directory provider is LookSmart (**www.looksmart.com**), which claims to have a directory of 1.5 million sites indexed into 100,000 categories. It has major players as partners, such as MSN, Netscape NetCenter, Time Warner, and Inktomi.

SEARCH ENGINES

A search engine consists of a database of sites on the internet, and software (known as spiders, crawlers, worms, or web robots) that endlessly trawl the internet collecting data to feed back to the database for processing and possible inclusion. Spiders also check out websites submitted to the search engine.

Author's new page is made available on the internet

The Internet

Author submits the same page to the search engine

The internet comprises the web, Usenet, newsgroups, business databases, Newsfeeds

Spiders visit web pages that have been submitted by authors and return data to the database

Spiders, unlike their organic counterparts, are searching the web 24 hours a day locating new data

Search Provider's database
Using the data returned by spiders, the search provider's database accumulates vast records of URLs related to their keywords

Users search the database by submitting search queries to the search engine

Searching the Links

Search engines collect information for their databases by using software called robots – which are more usually known as spiders or crawlers. Spiders trawl websites collecting information for the search providers' databases.

The information collected will usually vary between search providers. Most spiders find new web pages by following links within documents, and then links within the linked documents, and so on. It obviously doesn't take long to build up a collection of many thousands of URLs based on this simple principle. Different spiders collect different kinds of data from the web pages (and other information sources) they visit. Spiders are usually programmed to collect all or some of the following elements:

TITLES
The titles of individual web pages as defined by the web-page author.

CONTENT (INITIAL PARAGRAPHS)
The first few paragraphs of any web page.

META TAGS *(see below)*
Hidden content, as defined in META tags.

CONTENT (ENTIRE)
The entire contents of a web page.

META TAGS

META tags are lines of text hidden within a web page's HTML code. The META tags most commonly collected by spiders relate to keywords and description. By default, when a search engine give a description of a website in its list of hits, it shows the opening paragraphs of a web page. However, some search engines will replace this with the description you have specified within the Description META tag.

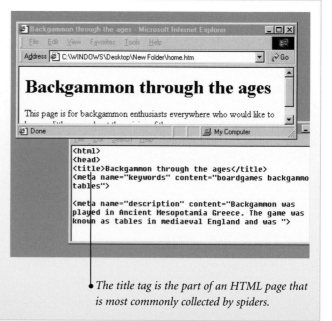

• *The title tag is the part of an HTML page that is most commonly collected by spiders.*

PROCESSING THE INFORMATION

● Having spidered a website, a search engine processes the information to ensure that searches return relevant hits.

● Some concentrate on the frequency and position of these keywords. Nearly all search engines look for keywords in the pages' titles, heads, subheads, and text in the first paragraphs.

FREQUENCY RATING

● These calculations help give the page a frequency rating for a term. Pages with a high frequency rating are at the top of lists of hits of searches for that term. The rating of pages is usually performed automatically.

RATING BY POPULARITY

● Services like Google base their ratings on a popularity system. A site linked to by many others is judged to be important, and if it is linked to by already important sites, the site is rated even higher.

● As the ranking of sites has no direct human involvement, Google can claim to be both spam- and bias-resistant.

METASEARCH PROGRAMS

Metasearch programs enable you to interrogate a number of search providers simultaneously, and offer both search engines and web directories.

Metasearch providers do not usually own or produce their own databases of websites and URLs. They provide the gateway for simultaneous searches to be carried out on the services with which they deal.

BROAD SEARCHES

● Metasearch programs can be extremely useful if you need to find out how much exists on the web on a particular topic. For broad searches, they are as useful as anything else on the web.

● The Metacrawler engine (**www.metacrawler.com**) searches 12 search engines and web directories by default. All you need to do is type your search query in the **What are you looking for?** text box and click on the **Search** button.

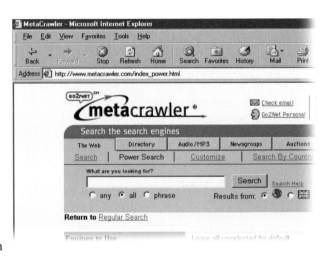

BUILT-IN METASEARCH

● The Microsoft search tool provided with Internet Explorer also has a metasearch option as one of its advanced features.

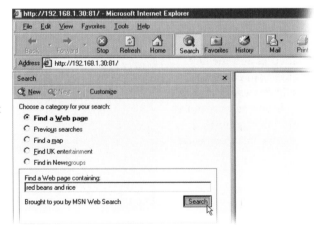

STANDALONE SEARCH PROGRAMS

It is likely that the next year or so will see a big increase in the popularity of *standalone* search agents – in other words, programs that you install on your computer and use as your main (or maybe your only) search tool.

COPERNIC 2000

● The example shown here, Copernic 2000 , functions in many ways as a metasearch engine. Search terms are highlighted in the hits list. Previous searches are saved, if required, in the top frame. This program also enables you to download documents or images for offline browsing.

● Updates are carried out automatically including information about engines and categories. Programs like Copernic do not necessarily offer anything that the best web-based search providers cannot offer. But their offline capabilities and the fact that they can connect directly to a wide range of information sources makes them a very interesting alternative for many users.

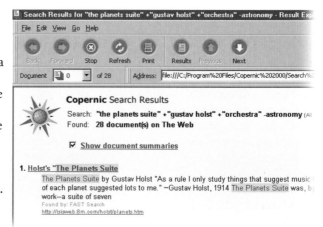

Selecting the software

USING SEARCH ENGINES

Ask a bookseller for a book on "entertainment" and you will get, at best, a perplexed frown. Similarly, search engines need a reasonably well-defined query to provide a useful response.

A BASIC SEARCH

Despite some similarities, search engines differ in the way they gather, handle, and deliver information. Nearly all search sites provide advanced search options – usually on separate *advanced search* pages. If you only intend to make a quick search, however, there are ways to modify your query so that you can type it into a standard search box and expect accurate results. In fact, many advanced menus are based on the few simple techniques described over the next few pages.

THE COMMONSENSE APPROACH

The first technique is not really a technique at all – just common sense. If you run a search and get results that are irrelevant, look at what went wrong with your search, then revise your query and resubmit it. You can make use of a first search to gather sufficient information to put together a second search simply by finding out what to include or exclude.

VAGUE SEARCH TERMS

Imagine someone would like to learn more about a piece of music, but all they know is that it comes from the orchestral work *The Planets*. A simple search for **the planets** is not likely to be very successful because the search term is way too broad and vague.

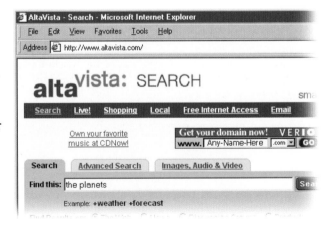

IRRELEVANT HITS

Using AltaVista
(www.altavista.com) to
search for **the planets**
returned nearly 95,000 hits,
but without anything
relevant in the first pages of
hits. The searcher needs to
narrow down the search.

RELATED TERMS

Usually a shot-in-the-dark
search can be useful in
providing a new angle for a
second search. The first
failed search could suggest
using a synonym for the
search term, or new words
to be added to the initial
search term. In this case,
nothing obvious occurs.
But adding a related term
like **orchestra** to the search
pays off immediately.

GETTING CLOSER

The search for **the planets**
and **orchestra** not only
reduces the number of hits
by one-third but, more
importantly, it brings the
most relevant hits to the
top of the list. The searcher
can now, if required,
compile further searches
using **Gustav Holst** as part
of the search query.

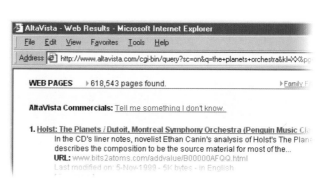

ADVANCED SEARCHING

Basic searches can be adequate for straightforward queries. However, you can greatly increase your chances of finding what you want on the web by knowing how to carry out more sophisticated searches. By learning some simple "grammar," you can have greater control over the way a search service responds to your requests. The majority of search services let you specify your search criteria in very precise ways, but different services provide these features in different ways.

SEARCH ENGINE MATH

Using math symbols can be the simplest and most effective way to broaden, or narrow, your search. They are accepted at almost every search engine on the web. The three main search modifiers you can use are:

+ (plus symbol)
- (minus symbol)
"..." (double quotation marks surrounding the search term)

+ SYMBOL

Use the + symbol to introduce additional search terms to your query. Place the + immediately before the additional search term (without leaving a space between them). In this example, **the planets +holst** will search for web pages that contain the words *the planets* and *holst*. This simple device reduces the number of hits from 950,000 to just over 130,000 with the most relevant at the beginning.

- SYMBOL

Use the - symbol to exclude words from your search, for example:
the planets -astronomy.
This searches for sites containing *the planets* but excludes those containing the word *astronomy*.

COMBINING SEARCH MATH

You can use the various search math queries in any combination. This will probably produce your most effective searches. For example: **gustav holst +the planets suite +orchestra -astronomy** yielded 87 web pages of hits – nearly all of them completely relevant.

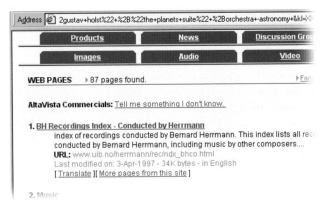

EXPERIMENT WITH SEARCH ORDER

As each search engine has its own way of handling queries, it is often worth experimenting with the order in which you submit your query. It doesn't seem logical that this should make much difference, but the search that returned only 87 pages in the previous example returned over 1300 when the order of the search terms were slightly altered.

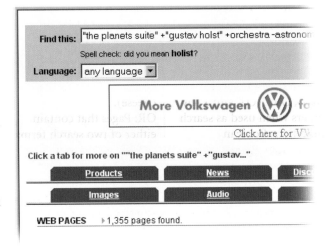

READ THE README

Search engine math, wildcards, and/or Boolean modifiers may not be universally accepted by search sites, but it is extremely rare for a search engine not to accept either + or AND or - or NOT. At least three search engines will not handle double quotations, and several more only accept wildcards and other options via their drop-down menu systems. If you don't get the results that these modifiers should provide, either read the advanced instructions for that provider, or simply move to a search engine that accepts them.

Double Quotes

Use the double quote marks around words to be grouped. If your query contains **the planets suite** the search engine will look for web pages containing those words as a phrase.

MORE SEARCH OPTIONS

Many search engines allow you to use an asterisk as a wildcard option in a search. This is useful if your search term has variant spellings. For example, you can type **mandol*** to cater for the two spellings: mandolin and mandoline, as well as including pages devoted to the mandola and mandolinists. It will also return hits for occurrences of the plural form, although most search engines automatically anticipate that you will be interested in plurals for your search terms.

BOOLEAN EXPRESSIONS

You will often encounter the phrase *Boolean modifiers* or *Boolean expressions*. These are essentially a technical way of describing the words AND, OR, NOT, and a few others when used as search modifiers. Boolean expressions are also commonly accepted by search engines, but on the whole you are safer using + (plus) rather than **AND**, and - (minus) rather than the modifier **NOT**. Some, but not all, search engines require you to use upper case when using Boolean logic. To be on the safe side, always use capital letters when entering Boolean expressions.

THE MODIFIERS: AND, NOT, OR, NEAR

AND: All search terms connected by AND will appear (i.e., bread AND cheese).
NOT: To exclude certain words (i.e., bread NOT cheese).
OR: Pages that contain either of two search terms (i.e., bread OR cheese)
NEAR Lets you specify (in numbers of characters) how near one search term is to another on a web page. This term is not widely accepted unless it is submitted as a menu option. The use of parentheses will allow you to group elements in your search. For example, NOT bread AND cheese means that pages with bread will be rejected but pages containing the word cheese will be returned. NOT (bread AND cheese) will avoid pages that contain both words.

Upper and lower case

By default, search engines look for your search query as upper case or lower case words. If you want to search specifically for upper case words, capitalize them in your search query. But the overwhelming majority of search engines will then look only for upper case occurrences of the search terms you have entered and ignore lower case variants.

DOMAIN NAME SEARCH

With this type of query you can specify that only a certain domain name is searched. For example, if you want to find information about Windows 98 straight from the developers, limit your search to microsoft.com by using the following syntax: **"Windows 98" domain:microsoft.com.**

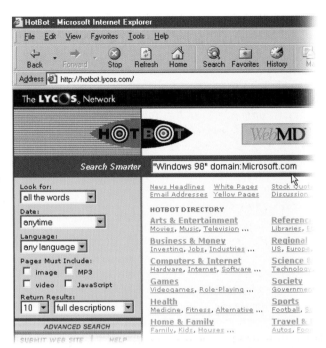

EXCLUSIVE LIST OF HITS

The resulting list of hits is confined exclusively to the numerous websites produced by Microsoft.

WEB RESULTS fewer than 100   1 - 10 next >>

1. Internet Explorer Products Download
Main download area for Microsoft Internet Explorer and rela
11/13/1999 http://www.microsoft.com/windows/ie/download/windows.htr
See results from this site only.

2. Microsoft Windows Update
Thank You for your interest in Windows Update Windows U
helps you get the most out of your computer. Windows®
the Windows Update service from the link on your...
9/12/1999 http://windowsupdate.microsoft.com/x86/w98/en/thanksstar
See results from this site only.

3. MSDN Online - Windows Logo Program
Adding the Windows Logo to your product indicates to you
tested to meet Microsoft standards for compatibility with V
to get the Windows Logo.
3/2/2000 http://msdn.microsoft.com/winlogo
See results from this site only.

You can also search for parts of the domain name, for example, to limit your search to sites that have the Australian identifier, type **"your search term" +domain:au.**

"Ayers Rock" +domain:au   `SEARCH`

Return to Fewer Options

Look For
Search for pages   all the words

USE THE ADVANCED OPTIONS

The following pages show how some of the leading search engines and web directories offer advanced features on their main search pages. These features achieve the same or similar results to using search engine math and Boolean operators, and often much more. The main search page of Hotbot (**www.hotbot.com**) offers all the features described so far. It also has an **Advanced Search** button that allows you to carry out even more detailed searches.

EASIER SEARCHING

It is unlikely that you will need to remember too many of these advanced search terms, other than ones we have looked at so far. Search sites are increasingly making life easier for users by providing useful drop-down menus, help files, check boxes, and other useful tools for users.

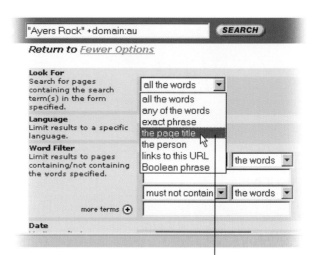

Many advanced features are made available through drop-down menus; in this example, a menu is conveniently placed near the search box and to the right of the directory lists

TITLE SEARCH

The title of a web page is determined by the words between the TITLE tags in the code of a web page. These words appear in the title bar at the top of the web browser. To search for web pages by title, use the following syntax: **title:your search term**. This option is unavailable in some search engines.

FORMAT-SPECIFIC SEARCHES

Many search providers supply useful radio buttons and check boxes near the main search box that enable you to specify the format for your search. For example, HotBot (address **hotbot.lycos.com**) has a check box that allows you to specify an images-only search. Here, a search is being carried out for royalty-free images.

• *The **image** check box*

LINKS SEARCH

A links search locates all web pages that contain hyperlinks to the specified web page. This is useful if you are interested in finding out how many people have linked their web pages to your own. The search syntax is: **link:yourwebpage.com**. As with title and domain searches, this advanced search is not accepted by all search engines.

The yellow search box at the top of the AltaVista web page (**www.altavista.com**) provides tabs that open pages for **Advanced Search** and **Images**, **Audio** and **Video** options. Clicking the **Advanced Search** tab reveals a number of useful options, including a **Language** box that enables you to specify the language in which the web page hits need to have been written, and two boxes (**From** and **To**) in which you can type a date range for your search.

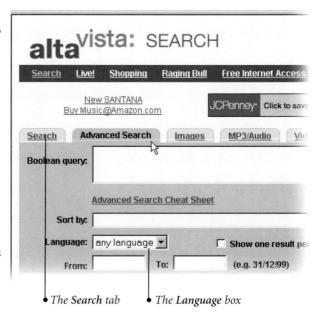

• *The Search tab*   • *The Language box*

The **Images, MP3/Audio**, and **Video** tabs at the top of the search box are useful for finding material in a particular format. Click the tab for the format you would like your search term to relate to, then click on the **Search** button.

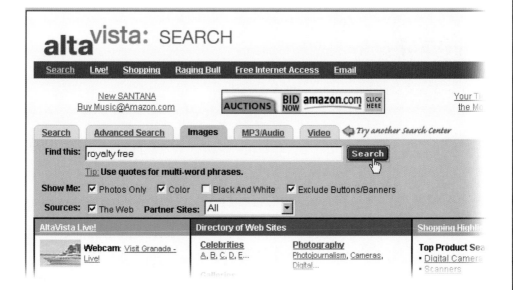

When presenting the results of a search for images, AltaVista doesn't only return a list of hits – it provides thumbnails of all the relevant images too. Click the thumbnail or the links beneath to go to the web page from which the image was retrieved, or to find similar images from other websites.

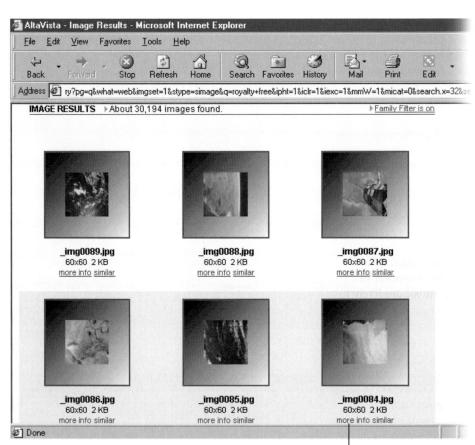

Click the links under any image to go to a web page

PICTURE FILE FORMATS

The letters .jpg after the images above shows that they are JPEG files. This compressed graphics file format is useful for images containing a lot of color. The GIF format, which you will also come across, is primarily used for displaying images from online sources such as the internet. It only supports 256 colors, but the files are small and can be used for animating web pages.

FROM ENGINES TO DIRECTORIES

The difference between search engines and web directories is becoming less distinct. It is now usual for search providers to offer a web directory as well as a search box on their main web page. To find information as quickly as possible, the search box and search menus are usually the place to begin. But for those who have a little more time to explore a subject, or who want results that have passed some kind of quality control, a directory can be preferable to a search engine.

This example shows one of the most popular web directories of all – Yahoo! (**www.yahoo.com**) – to look for information once more on Holst. The first stage involves some commonsense choices about the categories in which the composer or piece of music are likely to be found.

Computers & Internet
Internet, WWW, Software, Games...

Reference
Libraries, Dictionaries

Education
College and University, K-12...

Regional
Countries, Regions,

Entertainment
Cool Links, Movies, Humor, Music...

Science
Animals, Astronomy,

Government
Elections, Military, Law, Taxes...

Social Science
Archaeology, Econo

Health

Society & Cultu

http://www.yahoo.com/r/mu

After choosing a category, you can begin to refine your search by drilling down to a suitable subcategory. In this example, you might choose **Composition**, and then **Composers**.

- Chats and Forums *(212)*
- Classifieds *(10)* NEW!
- Collecting@
- Companies@
- Composition *(494)* NEW!
- Computer Generated *(311)*
- Contests, Surveys, Polls *(27)*
- Cover Art *(10)*

- Music Therapy@
- Music Videos *(31)*
- Musicology *(35)*
- New Releases *(5)*
- News and Media *(*
- Organizations *(255*
- Recording *(121)*
- Reference *(65)*

- Composers@
- Computer Generated@
- Interactive Operas@
- Lyrics and Notation *(195)* NEW!
- Organizations *(21)* NEW!

- Songwriting *(255)*
- Theory@
- FAQs *(1)*
- Usenet *(4)*

As you drill down further, the appropriate headings become more obvious. Holst is most likely to be found under the heading **Classical**. Eventually, you will find a list of websites that match your search requirements.

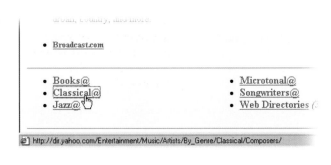

Here, the search has reached the end of the directory entries and has reached a website dedicated to classical composers.

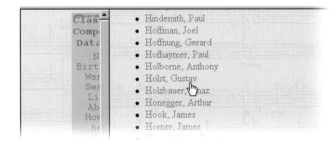

The extensive list of classical composers available on this website confirms that you have reached what you are looking for: a large database of composers that contains an entry for **Holst, Gustav**.

Finally, you have arrived at a biography of Gustav Holst. The principal advantage of using a directory search rather than entering keywords in a search box is that you are presented with many more related options that you can examine during the search. This may lead you to information related to your areas of interest that a straightforward keyword search may not.

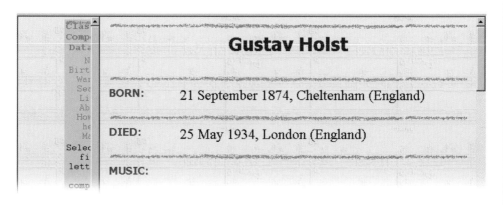

STANDALONE SEARCH PROGRAMS

The latest generation of search software runs directly from your computer rather than via a website. The free search program Copernic 2000 (available from the website **www.copernic.com**), is a powerful metasearch tool with some very useful customizable features. For example, it can update automatically its list of search engines while you are browsing. It also enables you to download search results for offline browsing, and will remove duplicates for you.

---

171 **Selecting the software**

WHICH SEARCH ENGINE?

This chapter looks at nine of today's most popular search providers describing the main features and showing the web page layout and the results format for each.

WHY CHOOSE BETWEEN THEM?

You might wonder if there is any need to go looking for another search provider once you have found one that suits your needs. The simple answer is no – as long as you are happy with the accuracy, quality, and currency of the results that the provider returns, and the speed of delivery and the ease of use.

SEVERAL PROVIDERS
Nevertheless, it is advisable to bookmark several web directories and search engines for these reasons:
1 Different search providers almost never return identical results.
2 Search providers can present the results of a search in a variety of very different ways.

Different results
*As the examples opposite show, the same query ("**gustav holst**" +"**the planets suite**" +**orchestra -astronomy**) submitted to different search engines can return different lists of hits. The next chapter explains why these differences in the order and content of the results occur, by looking at how search engines and web directories work.*

WHY SEARCHES GO WRONG

The roots of this problem lie in the two methods used to compile databases – by keyword or by concept. Keyword searches collect words in a site that are thought to be important. The problem arises when you enter a word with more than one meaning. If you enter the word "groom," you will be offered sites on horse care and weddings. Concept searches try to work out the meaning of the text rather than just using the specific words. Problems arise when the software working out the meaning of an article containing the word "heart" places it in a medical category when the subject is love.

ALTAVISTA

Opened in 1995, AltaVista is one of the largest web search engines and contains an index of more than 31 million web pages. It has a multilingual search capability using its own *Babel Fish* translation software. This service, which was the first of its kind to be used on the net, can translate words, phrases, and entire sites.

RESULTS FORMAT

Results include page title, description, date, and options to view more pages from the same site or have the information translated. Other information (e.g., Company factsheet) is offered where appropriate.

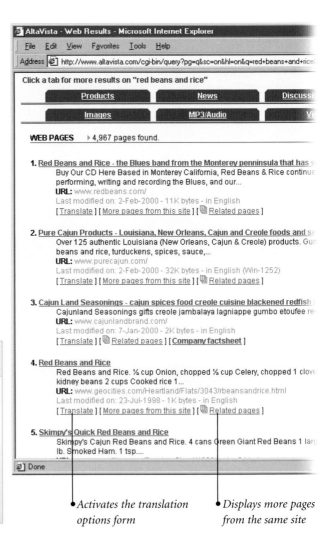

• *Activates the translation options form*

• *Displays more pages from the same site*

ALTAVISTA FEATURES

- www.altavista.com
- Very large database.
- Online instructions available.
- Relevance to query used to rank results.
- Compact or detailed display of results.

Multimedia search features
(images, audio and, video tabs)•

Drop-down menu for
language options •

• Family filter

Advanced •
Search tab

Search box •

Radio •
buttons to
specify search
areas

Directory •
data – mainly
provided by
the Open
Directory
Project

Help files •
and company
information

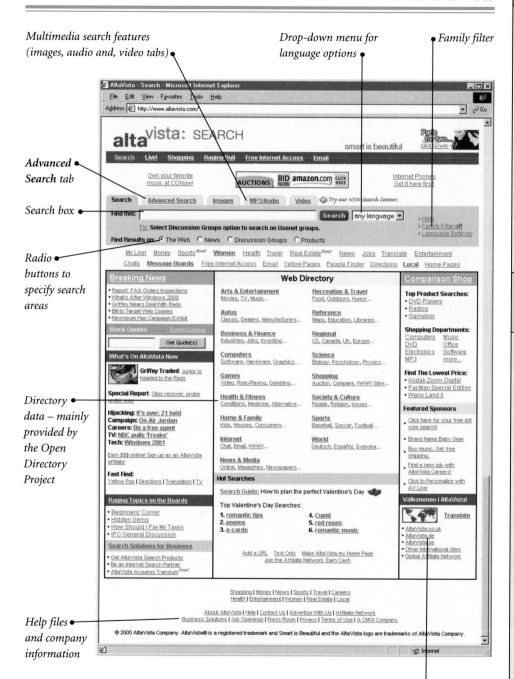

International sites and translation options •

ASK JEEVES

Ask Jeeves is one of several internet search engines that supports *natural language* queries. Ask Jeeves a question and he will return a list of hits organized into drop-down lists of related sites. Unlike other similar search engines, though, Ask Jeeves provides answers in the form of questions that it hopes will exactly match what you are looking for. According to its owners, every link in the Ask Jeeves knowledge base has been selected by an editor, not by an automated process.

RESULTS FORMAT

Whether your search is a question in plain English or a sequence of words, the answers from Ask Jeeves are in the form of questions. Otherwise, hits for your search term will be organized in further drop-down menus – one for each search engine that has been interrogated.

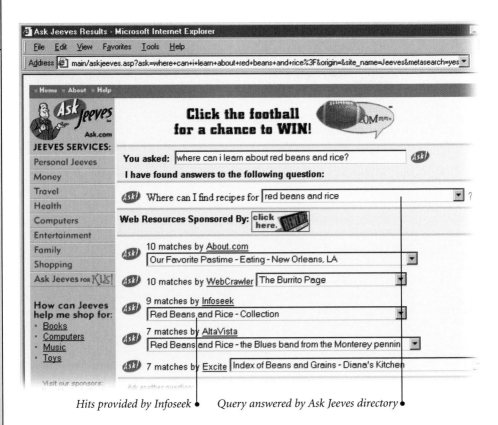

Hits provided by Infoseek •   *Query answered by Ask Jeeves directory* •

ASK JEEVES FEATURES

- **www.askjeeves.com**
- Queries can be made in natural language.
- Main search provided by Ask Jeeves directory.

- Unknown spellings are queried and a spell check is offered.
- Secondary search (a *metasearch* feature)

interrogates leading search engines.
- **Personal Jeeves** feature offers customized information and services.

Type your query as a plain English question (or simply a word, or a string of words) •

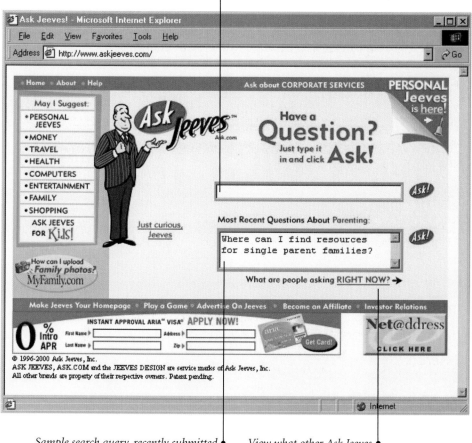

Sample search query, recently submitted •

View what other Ask Jeeves • *users are searching for now*

DOGPILE

Dogpile is among the most popular metasearch engines – an engine that sequentially queries several search engines and web directories. It can access 18 information sources, such as stock prices, yellow pages, and weather forecasts. Information from Usenet newsgroups and other information sources is also available.

CONTROLLING THE SEARCH

Dogpile presents results grouped under individual search providers. Rather than simultaneously interrogating all the search providers, Dogpile submits your query to a selection of providers at a time. Dogpile's advanced search feature enables you to determine the order in which these sources are queried, and to remove information sources from its metasearch list if they are not relevant to your query. By checking the appropriate radio button below the search box, you can specify a search area before hitting the **Fetch** button. After reading the list of hits, you can tell Dogpile to query more search providers by clicking on **Next Set of Search Engines** at the foot of the page.

DOGPILE FEATURES

- **www.dogpile.com**
- Easily customized.
- Large number and variety of information

sources queried.
- Useful regional feature for searching locally.
- Specify information

source-type before beginning search.
- Also offers directory structure for searching.

Specify the type of
information to be retrieved •

Click this tab to set your regional preferences, type
• your City, State and/or Zip Code, and click *Save*

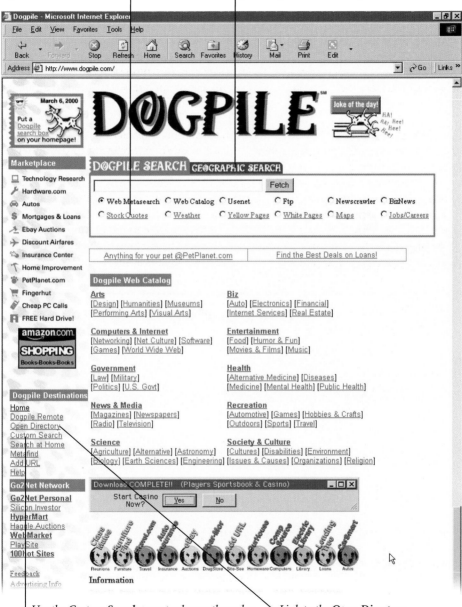

• Use the **Custom Search** page to change the order
in which the specified search engines are queried

• Link to the **Open Directory**
(Dogpile version)

GOOGLE

Google's main search page is in stark contrast to the busy portal interface favored by many top search providers.

However, behind the simple, uncluttered interface a very powerful search engine using unique software is at work.

PAGE RANKING

Google's search engine is based on an automated method that ranks web pages according to their relationship with other web pages – with special attention being paid to the links between pages that share common subjects or themes. Google analyzes the relevance of a page by looking at the pages that link to it. Each link is regarded as a "vote" for that page, and the more votes a page receives, the more highly it is ranked.

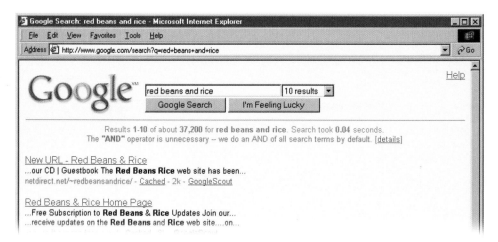

SEARCH TERMS AND PROXIMITY

Google only produces results that match all your search terms. It also notes the proximity of the search terms on a page, and prioritizes those hits that place the search terms close to each other.

"I'm feeling lucky"

The developers at Google are very confident of the effectiveness of Google's search capabilities, and they have incorporated a unique feature in their **I'm Feeling Lucky** button.

If you click on this button after entering your search terms, Google will send you straight to the website that emerges at the top of its search results, and many times it is uncannily accurate.

*Google's **I'm feeling lucky** button runs your search and then takes you straight to the web page of the number one hit*

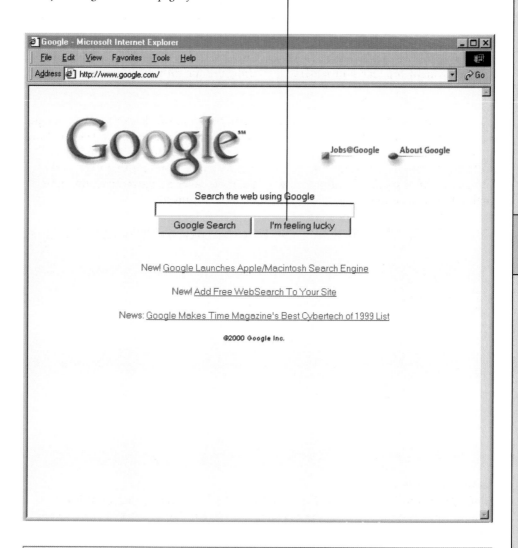

GOOGLE FEATURES

- **www.google.com**
- Minimalist, uncluttered search screen.

- Has the unique **I'm Feeling Lucky** button for fast results.

- Has its own software for rating pages.
- Matches all terms used.

HOTBOT

HotBot has been one of the leading search engines since its launch by Wired Digital in 1996. While essentially a search engine, it now provides a directory service using material mainly from the Open Directory. HotBot has proved enormously popular in recent years because of its highly effective user interface. From the main search page, it is easy to fine-tune a search using the drop-down menus in the left-hand panel. With most search engines, you need to access a separate page to set these advanced options. HotBot is also capable of processing plain English queries.

Along with the list of hits, HotBot offers a number of search refinements and other related information likely to be useful to the searcher. In this case, it offers a link to down-loadable music files on the LycosMusic service.

Automatic search refinements

Advanced Search options tab

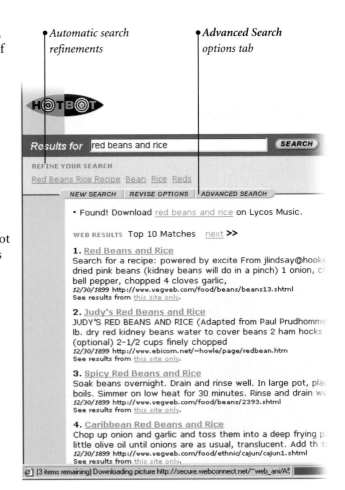

THE LYCOS NETWORK

Since October 1998 HotBot has been part of the Lycos network and is run as a separate service on this network, which offers numerous Net-based services including free email, clubs, chat, a shopping center, and entertainment.

HOTBOT FEATURES

- **www.hotbot.com**
- Many power-searching options available via

drop-down menus from the main interface.
- Indexes more than 110

million web documents.
- Offers natural language construction of searches.

Many advanced search options are available from these drop-down menus

Free email and home pages on offer

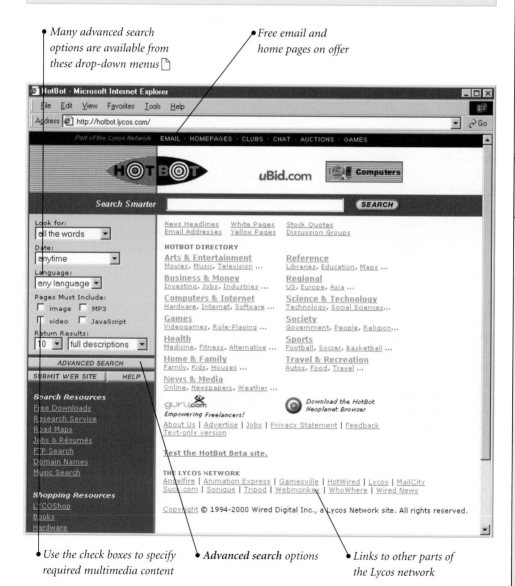

Use the check boxes to specify required multimedia content

***Advanced search** options*

Links to other parts of the Lycos network

135 Use the Advanced Options

LYCOS

Lycos began as a search engine but now boasts a very large directory (with some excellent multimedia areas), which is its primary asset. Its portal interface makes Lycos similar in structure and overall feel to Yahoo! From the main Lycos page you can set up a free email account, organize free internet access, play online games, chat online, build your own home page, read news headlines, and much more. You can also customize the Lycos page to suit your own preferences.

SEARCH RESULTS

These are usefully organized by categories: first by the most popular links, then websites (results mainly drawn from the Open Directory), news articles (from some of the web's top news sites) and finally shopping (with results from LYCOShop).

IMAGE GALLERY

The excellent searchable image gallery contains more than 80,000 picture files, viewable initially as thumbnails. You can also use Lycos to search the web specifically for images, audio or video files.

*The **Popular** heading appears when the Lycos search team have gathered sites appropriate for this search.*

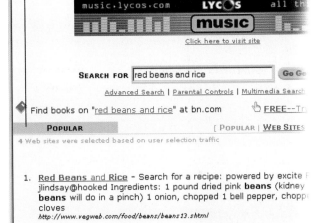

Online help

Lycos provides detailed help files for searching, and for viewing and downloading files in its Image Gallery.

LYCOS FEATURES

- **www.lycos.com**
- This is a powerful search site with many customizable features.
- **Safe search** parental control feature.
- Searchable Lycos image gallery and multimedia search feature for the entire web.

The **Tools** option lets you specify the areas that you want to be searched

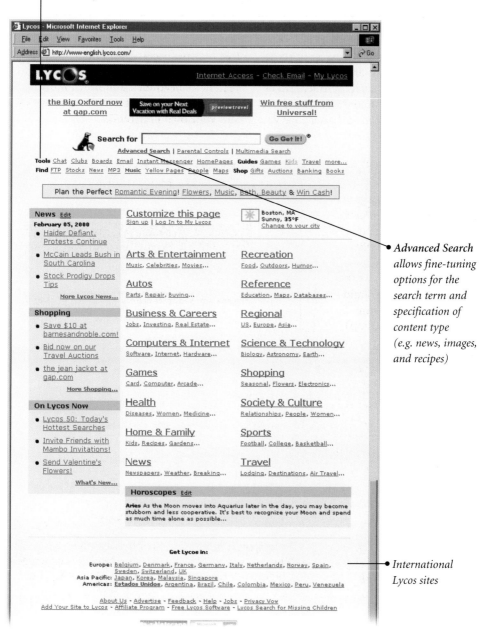

Advanced Search allows fine-tuning options for the search term and specification of content type (e.g. news, images, and recipes)

International Lycos sites

METACRAWLER

Metacrawler is another major metasearcher from the Lycos network, but unlike Dogpile it presents the results according to relevance, site, or source. MetaCrawler gets its results from a large number of web search engines. It then collates the results and presents them in one long list of hits, arranged according to preferences that are specified in the order of the search terms entered by the user.

WIDEN OR NARROW THE SEARCH

Metacrawler gives the source of the results and provides a brief description of the site of each search provider that has returned a hit. There is also a link to other search providers. A **View Related** feature provides further possible hits as well as an option to narrow the search to various types of search formats.

• *Metacrawler suggests refinements for your search*

• *Email results to a friend option*

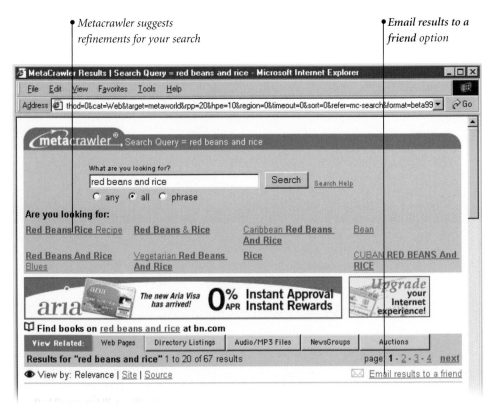

Choose information source-type

Metaspy is a fun feature that lets you take a peek at what other Metacrawler users are searching for at that moment

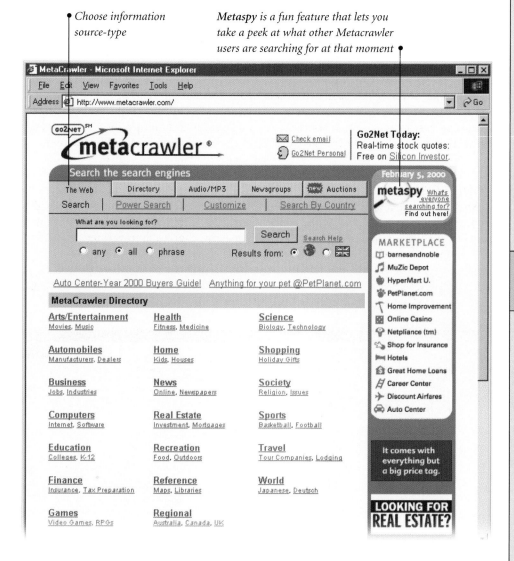

METACRAWLER FEATURES

- www.metacrawler.com
- Create your own customized search page.
- Any duplicate returns are eliminated.
- Offers **Search by country** feature.
- The MiniCrawler feature is a small desktop window of MetaCrawler.
- MetaSpy feature shows other users' queries.

NETSCAPE SEARCH

To access Netscape Search's search page, click **Search Shortcuts** at center-top of the Netscape home page. This all-in-one search page gives easy access to more than 30 different search providers organized according to search type.

SPECIALIST SEARCHES

Netscape's search pages include specialist search providers such as WhoWhere (**www.whowhere.com**) for locating people, and e-commerce-related search tools (such as **wine.com**). Netscape's search service returns four distinct types of data to a search query: websites, NetCenter pages (relating to content within Netscape NetCenter), website categories (relating to categories within the Open Directory project), and Reviewed websites.

NETSCAPE SEARCH FEATURES

- **www.netscape.com**
- Directory-based engine built by human editors.
- Internet Keywords feature allows quick location of companies' websites simply by entering company name.
- Comprehensive help files available.
- Regularly scanned for dead links.

Click a search provider to activate it for the current search

Check this box to make the current search service the default

Your search term is remembered when you return to this page either to modify the search or to use another service

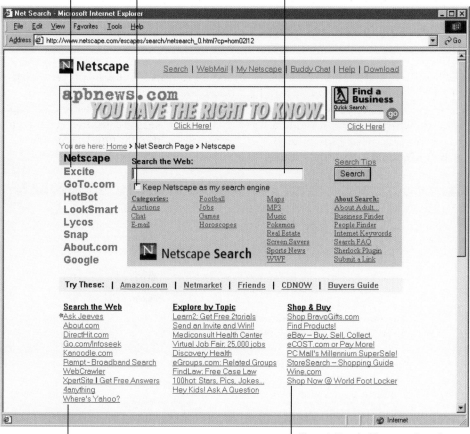

Netscape Search offers a wide range of alternative search services

Shop & Buy in Netscape Search provides a comprehensive shopping opportunity

NORTHERN LIGHT

Northern Light boasts a special collections database comprising over 6000 publications. All information sources are fully searchable so that any successful query will produce a summary of results with appropriate source details.

NORTHERN LIGHT'S CUSTOM SEARCH FOLDERS

Northern Light groups the results of your queries in folders to the left of the browser window. These Custom Search Folders are unique to your search rather than representing the search provider's own web directory categories.

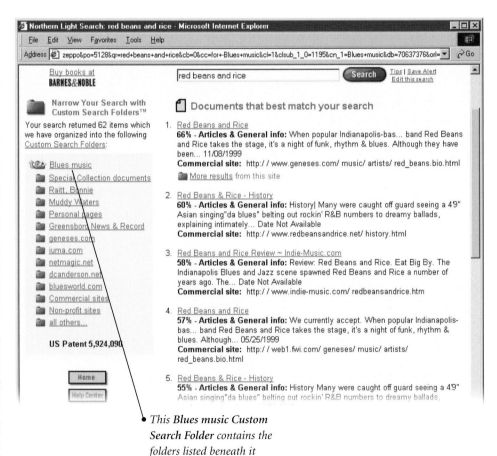

*This **Blues music Custom Search Folder** contains the folders listed beneath it*

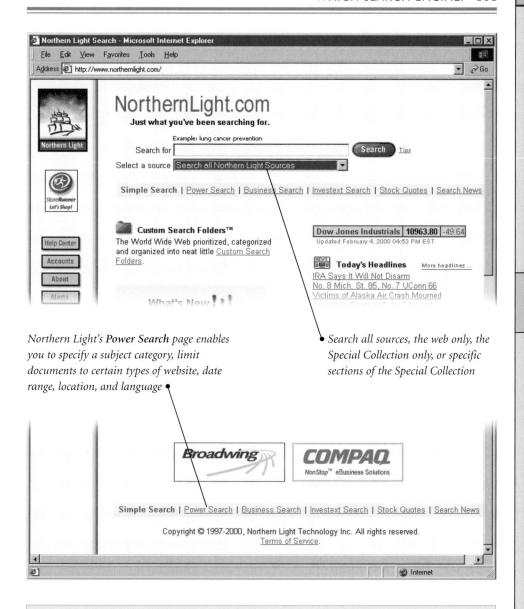

*Northern Light's **Power Search** page enables you to specify a subject category, limit documents to certain types of website, date range, location, and language*

Search all sources, the web only, the Special Collection only, or specific sections of the Special Collection

NORTHERN LIGHT FEATURES

● Supports queries made in natural language.
● **northernlight.com**

● Special set of over 1600 documents unavailable elsewhere on the web.

● Custom search folders group returned hits by subject category.

SPECIALIZED SEARCHES

The availability of information and products on the web has led to the development of countless sites where you can find people, services, news, and software, which we look at here.

ADVANCED OPTIONS

As we have seen in previous chapters, all the most popular search engines provide much more than the basic tools for searching the web. Nearly all offer advanced options that enable you to search specifically for email addresses, Usenet newsgroup postings, information from news feeds, white and yellow pages, shopping databases, software collections, maps, online shopping, and auctions.

DATABASE INTERROGATION

Since all this information is held on databases owned and maintained by search providers, the source of the material – whether web, Usenet newsgroup, or commercial telephone listings – is irrelevant. When you run a search from your web browser you are not running a live search of what is on the internet at that moment, but rather interrogating a database owned by that particular search provider. Some search providers, however, specialize in certain types of information, which we look at in the next few pages.

SEARCHING FOR PEOPLE

Email directories and white pages services are still in their infancy and are not yet fully comprehensive. This means that there is no guarantee you'll find that long-lost neighbor who moved away years ago.

However, if your old neighbor signed up for a free email account and, while doing so, left the box that says **include me in your email directory** checked, he/she may certainly be listed in at least one email directory.

Other providers
Email addresses and white pages data are available as search options from many search providers. You can also run a people search from Microsoft Outlook or Outlook Express.

OUTLOOK EXPRESS

Although Microsoft's email program, Outlook Express, is not primarily a tool for searching the web, it does include a **Find People** feature. You can use it to find people either locally in your own address book or globally on the internet.

1 OUTLOOK EXPRESS
● In Outlook Express, click on the **Addresses** button in the toolbar.

2 FIND PEOPLE
● In the **Address Book** window, click on the **Find People** button.

3 SEARCH PROVIDER
● Choose a search provider from the drop-down menu. In this example, the Lycos Network's **WhoWhere? Internet Directory Service** is being used.

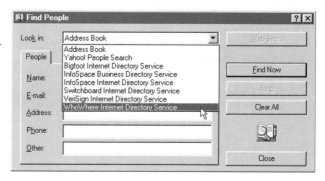

4 FIND NOW
● Type the name of the person you are searching for and click on **Find Now**.

5 BROWSE THE NAMES

● After a short wait, a list of names is compiled for you to browse.

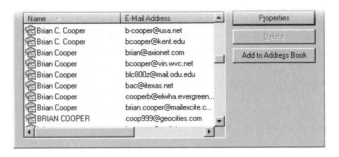

BIGFOOT

Bigfoot (**www.bigfoot.com**) is renowned for its simplicity as a people finder. You can enter just the first and last names of the person you're looking for. However, it also offers a number of options for narrowing down the terms of your search.

1 STARTING THE NAME SEARCH

● Type the name of the person you're looking for, and specify a city if you want to make the search more specific.

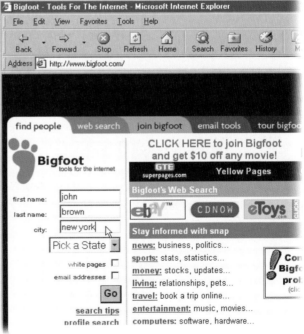

2 PICKING A STATE

● Click the arrow next to **Pick a State** and choose the relevant state from the menu that appears.

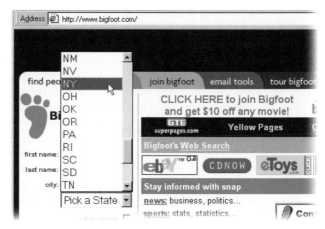

3 CLICKING ON GO

● Check the box next to white pages, email addresses, or both. Then click on **Go**.

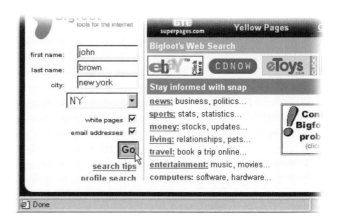

4 DISPLAYING THE RESULTS

● Results appear grouped under email addresses or as white pages entries with the telephone numbers of the people found.

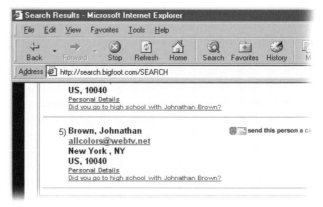

YELLOW PAGES

With the vast explosion in commercial websites – from one-person startups right up to multinationals – and the rise of ecommerce, there has been a corresponding growth on the web of search sites devoted to finding businesses, their products and services, and the people who make them work.

COMMERCIAL SEARCHES

Once again, many of the main search services provide a perfectly adequate method of searching for such material. All you have to do is choose the yellow pages or white pages (or people or businesses) options and then run your search as usual via the search box.

However, if your favorite search service doesn't give you this option, you could go straight to a search provider who specializes in commercial searches. GTE Superpages.com (**www.superpages.com**) offers an immensely wide range of search options for people, companies, services, products, and much more.

In the example that we are working through on these pages, however, we are using Ameritech.yellowpages.net (**www.yellowpages.net**) to find out where we could eat an Italian meal during our upcoming trip to Seattle.

1 APPROPRIATE CATEGORY

● Enter **restaurants** in the **Category** box, **Seattle** in the **City** box, select **Washington** from the **State** drop-down menu, and finally click on **Find it!**

The Category box ●────

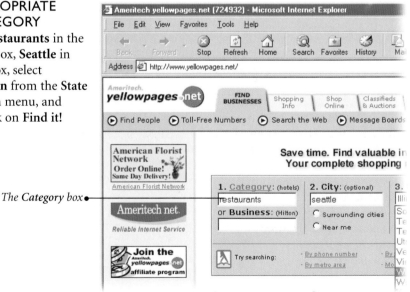

2 RELATED CATEGORIES

● Scroll down the list of hits. At the bottom, a list of **Related Categories** appears. Click the appropriate category – in this case, **Restaurants-Italian**.

3 FURTHER INFORMATION

● Click on any restaurant in the list for further information and a map.

A-Z list of Italian restaurants

SEARCHING FOR NEWS

To search for postings to Usenet newsgroups, use the Usenet option in your favorite search service, if available. This is sometimes accessed via the Advanced search settings, but different search services use different locations.

SIMPLY DOGPILE

In the case of Dogpile, (**www.dogpile.com**), simply click the **Usenet** radio button before clicking on **Fetch** to run your search.

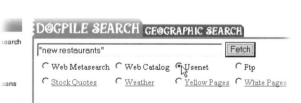

USENET SEARCH

Along with a number of other search services, product details, and a web index, Deja.com offers a vast searchable database of Usenet newsgroup messages including archive material going back several years.

Results are clearly organized making it easy to follow discussion threads within and across the tens of thousands of available newsgroups. Searching for Usenet messages can be as easy as searching the web.

1 POWER SEARCHING

● Deja.com's usenet service is available on **deja.com/usenet**. On this web page, click on **Power Search**. (Unless you have an extremely specific query, using **Quick Search** usually returns too many hits.)

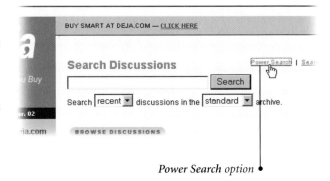

Power Search option ●

2 ENTERING KEYWORDS

● On the **Power Search** page, type your query in the **Enter Keywords** box. Explore the options in the drop-down menus under **Limit Search** and choose any that seem appropriate, then click on **Search**.

Type your keyword here ●

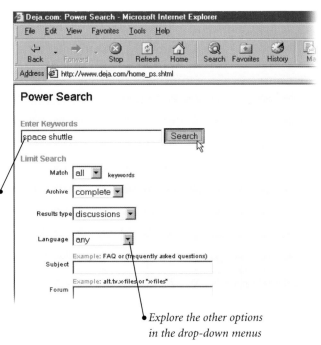

● *Explore the other options in the drop-down menus*

3 READING THE MESSAGE

● When the list of hits appears, click the messages you wish to read. The date of posting, the name of the Usenet newsgroup, and the name of the author also appear in the same line.

List of hits ●

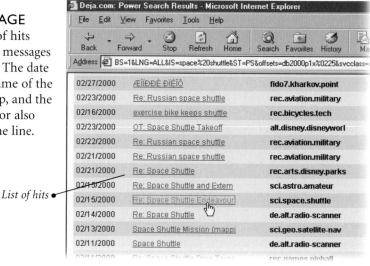

4 CHOOSING THE OPTIONS

● After reading the message, choose from the list of options below the message, or move to the next or previous message in the list of hits.

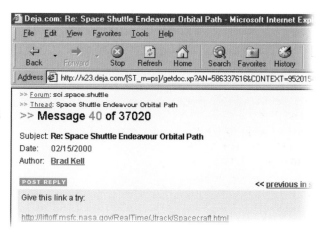

CLASSIFICATIONS OF POSTINGS

Usenet postings can fall into one of the following classifications:
alt. Anything goes
rec. Recreational topics

comp. Computer subjects
soc. Social issues
sci. Science subjects
news. Usenet information
biz. Business matters

humanities. The arts
talk. Current debates
regional. Local subjects
k12. Educational issues
misc. The unclassifiable.

SEARCHING FOR SOFTWARE

If you are interested in searching for a particular piece of software, simply browsing to see what utilities or patches are available, or looking for a certain game, there are many excellent shareware and freeware sites on the web that will almost certainly have what you want. Most contain a search box and a site directory structure that is as simple to use as any standard search engine.

SIMPLY BROWSING

If you are interested in checking out the latest internet search software available for Windows, for example, you can simply browse the relevant section of a software download site like **www.winfiles.com**.

1 CHOOSING A CATEGORY
● On the main page of Winfiles.com, click on **Windows Shareware**.

Choose a category ●

2 DRILLING ON DOWN
● In the next window we again choose the category we are looking for, in this case **Windows 95/98 Software**, so we click on it.

3 WORKING THROUGH THE LEVELS

● After clicking on **Network and Internet Tools** (below), we select **Web Browser Tools.**

Network and Internet Tools

Web Browser Tools

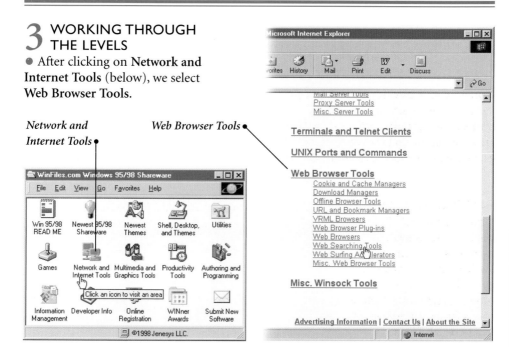

4 SELECTING THE SOFTWARE

● Scroll down the list of shareware descriptions until you find something that interests you. This example shows the **Copernic2000** program.

Download time

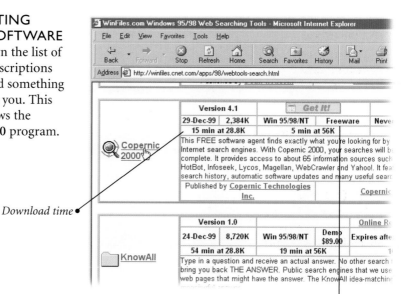

This shows the program's shareware status – in this case it is freeware

USING THE SEARCH BOX

If you know the name of the piece of software you want to download, use the search box provided at the software site.

For example, to find and download the popular email client, Eudora Light, from the Tucows software site, do the following:

1 TYPING THE SEARCH TERM

● Go to Tucows' website (**www.tucows.com**). In the **Search Tucows** window type the search term: **Eudora Light**. If necessary, click on an entry in the menu in the right-hand box to specify your PC's operating system.

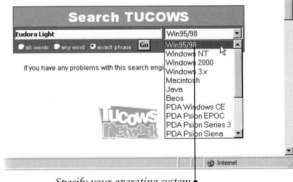

Specify your operating system ●

2 CLICKING ON EXACT PHRASE

● Click the **Exact phrase** radio button to search for the complete phrase **Eudora Light**, and click the **Go** button.

3 DOWNLOAD NOW

● Click the **Download Now** button next to the appropriate description. Follow the instructions that appear onscreen regarding download and installation.

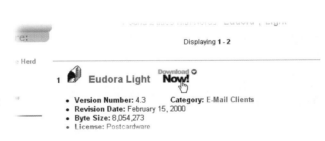

4 CHOOSING A REGIONAL SITE

● Choose a regional site closest to you from which to download.

To ensure faster and more reliable downloads, please choose
a site within the continent or region closest to you.
⌐ would like to learn more about the benefits of hosting a TUCOWS affiliate site, **click** h
Welcome to TUCOWS, the world's best collection of Internet Software.

Please select the country you live in (or the one nearest you).

Pick a Region:

Africa
Asia
Australia
Canada
Caribbean
Central America
Europe
South America
United States

Continue...

5 CHOOSING A LOCAL SITE

● Specify the site most local to you from which the software is available.

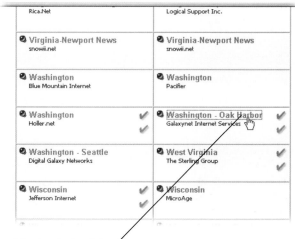

Rica.Net	Logical Support Inc.
🌐 **Virginia-Newport News** snowii.net	🌐 **Virginia-Newport News** snowii.net
🌐 **Washington** Blue Mountain Internet	🌐 **Washington** Pacifier
🌐 **Washington** Holler.net	🌐 **Washington - Oak Harbor** Galaxynet Internet Services
🌐 **Washington - Seattle** Digital Galaxy Networks	🌐 **West Virginia** The Sterling Group
🌐 **Wisconsin** Jefferson Internet	🌐 **Wisconsin** MicroAge

Selecting the local site ●

6 MONITORING THE DOWNLOAD

● If the download utility **Netzip Download Demon** is installed on your computer, its window opens to monitor the downloading. Once the software is downloaded, it's yours to use.

EMAIL

E MAIL is an easy-to-follow guide to Microsoft's email program, Outlook Express. This section can be used by people with very little experience with Outlook Express. Outlook Express's essential features are presented in a clear and simple order that allows easy understanding of their functions and how to carry them out. The first chapter shows you how to launch the Outlook Express program and explains the toolbars. In the next chapter, step-by-step sequences show you how to compose messages, attach files, and send email. In the final chapter of this section, you will find out how to check for new messages, read them, save attachments, and organize your mail on your PC.

OUTLOOK EXPRESS

Outlook Express is part of Microsoft's Internet Explorer web browser suite of programs. It offers all the features you need to be able to send and receive electronic mail over the internet.

WHAT OUTLOOK EXPRESS CAN DO

Outlook Express provides a gateway to the world of electronic mail. It allows you to send 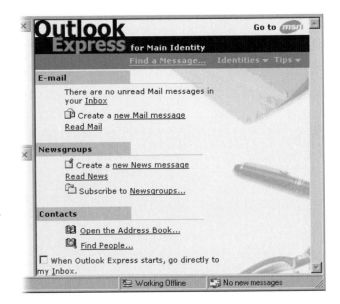 and receive electronic mail messages, and it provides facilities for you to record and store all your email addresses and personal contact details, in the form of an electronic address book.

Outlook Express has the additional benefit that if there are other people who wish to use your computer to receive their own email, you can create multiple user identities so that their email and contact details can be kept separately and privately from your own.

EMAIL
Email is the main activity provided by Outlook Express. It provides a user-friendly interface that makes it easy to compose, send, and receive email messages directly from the main window. Email messages can contain text, pictures, hypertext links to websites, and even self-contained file attachments.

Sending
Emails

Receiving
Emails

NEWSGROUPS

For those who have mastered the art of sending email and want to branch out into the world of online debate and discussion, Outlook Express provides a newsreading facility that enables you to read and join in with electronic "newsgroups." Newsgroup discussions cover just about every topic under the sun, from world politics and all types of hobbies and leisure interests to more focused subjects, such as the life cycle of the dung beetle or sea turtle conservation.

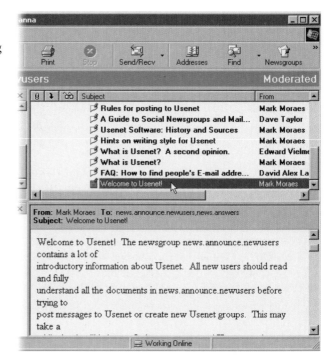

CONTACTS

Using the Outlook Express address book you can build up an electronic database of personal and business contacts. For each contact you can record name, home, business, personal, and other details. You can then use these address book records to address emails without having to retype the address each time. The address book helps you to manage your email sessions more efficiently.

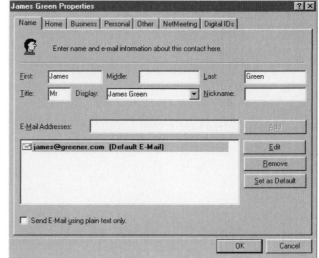

LAUNCHING OUTLOOK EXPRESS

Outlook Express can be started, or "launched" from either the Windows **Start** menu, directly from the desktop (if the Outlook Express shortcut has been placed on the desktop), or from within Microsoft's Internet Explorer program itself. Follow the steps to launch the program using any of these methods.

FROM THE DESKTOP

To launch Outlook Express from the desktop:
● Locate the **Outlook Express** shortcut icon. This has the appearance of an envelope with two blue arrows encircling it, and the words **Outlook Express** are written beneath it.
● Position the mouse pointer over the Outlook Express icon and double-click the left mouse button to launch the program.

FROM THE START MENU

To launch Outlook Express from the Start Menu:
● Click on the **Start** button.
● Move the mouse pointer to **Programs** in the Start menu and the **Programs** submenu is displayed.
● Move the mouse pointer across to **Outlook Express** on the **Programs** submenu and click once. Outlook Express begins to run.

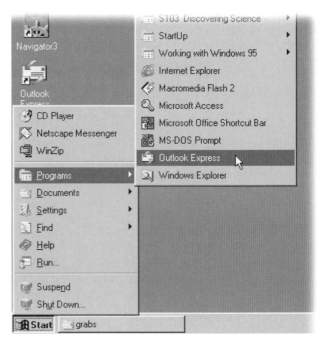

FROM INTERNET EXPLORER

When Internet Explorer is open, you can open Outlook Express directly from Explorer's Mail menu.

● Click on the **Mail** button on the main Internet Explorer toolbar.

● Select the option that you require from the drop-down menu.

● Outlook Express is launched, showing a new message window, or the **Inbox**, depending on the menu option you selected from the menu.

THE OUTLOOK EXPRESS PANEL

Once the program has started up, the Outlook

Express window ⛶ appears showing the Outlook Express panel on the left. This panel has shortcuts to

some features of the program, such as creating new email messages and opening the Address Book.

The Outlook ●
Express window

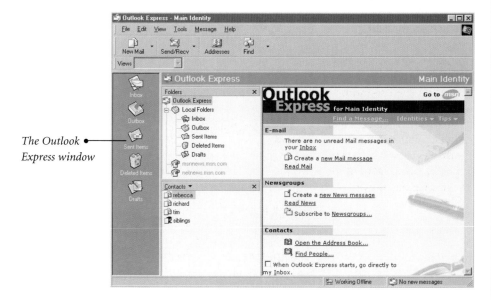

THE OUTLOOK EXPRESS WINDOW

The Outlook Express window is divided into different sections, some of which are visible only when you perform actions they relate to. You can personalize the Outlook Express window to display as many or few of these sections as you wish.

WINDOW PANELS

❶ Outlook Bar
The Outlook bar provides handy shortcuts to some of the key folders. You can customize the Outlook bar to include the folders that you use most frequently.

❷ Contacts Panel
This panel displays a list of all the contacts that are stored in the current user's Address Book.

❸ Folders Panel
A folder can be selected in this panel to become the currently active folder whose contents are displayed in the main area of the window.

❹ Folders List
This shows all the folders and subfolders in which the current user's email and newsgroup messages have been saved and stored.

❺ Views Bar
The views bar allows you to show or hide different categories of messages according to your choice.

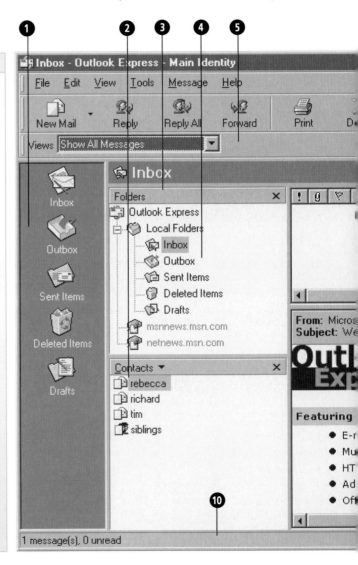

THE MENU BAR

The Menu bar, just below the Title bar at the top of the screen, contains some menu options, such as **File** and **Edit**, that are shared with other Microsoft programs and may be familiar. However, the **Message** option, through which messages are controlled, is unique to Outlook Express.

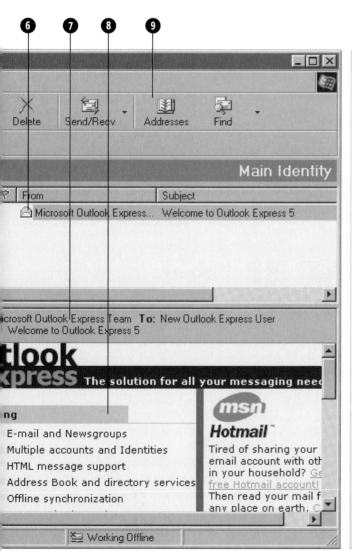

WINDOW PANELS

6 Message List
This shows a list of all the messages that are contained in the active folder (the folder that has been selected from the Folder list or Outlook bar).

7 Preview Panel Header
Contains summary information about the currently selected message.

8 Preview Panel
The contents of the selected message in the Message List can be read here.

9 Toolbar
The bar at the top of your screen displays buttons enabling you to access Outlook's main features quickly and easily. The items on the toolbar change depending on which part of the program you are using.

10 Status Bar
Displays information about activities that you perform and the status of your internet connection.

182 **The toolbar buttons**

THE TOOLBAR

The toolbar for the Outlook Express window provides access to some of the main features of Outlook Express. You can initiate most of your sending and receiving from the toolbar and perform activities, such as printing and deleting messages, and searching for items in your mail folders. As you move from one folder to the next, the buttons on the toolbar change. For example, when you first launch Outlook Express only four buttons are on the toolbar, but when you go to the Inbox more appear. At times, some of the buttons appear grayed-out because that particular function is not available from that window at that time.

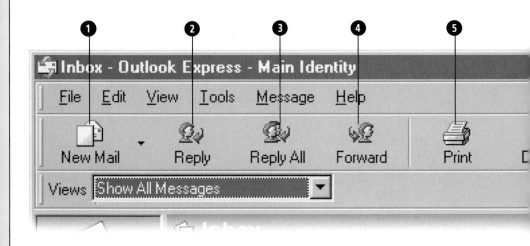

THE TOOLBAR BUTTONS

1 New Mail
This button opens a blank email message window. By clicking on the arrow to the right of this button, you can open a template containing a design – for a birthday or an invitation – in which you can type your message.

2 Reply
You can reply to any message in the Inbox by clicking on this button. A new message window opens with the address of the sender already filled in.

3 Reply All
By clicking on this button you can circulate a reply that is sent to both the sender and the other

recipients of a message in your Inbox. A new message window opens with the address of the sender and all the other recipients, including yourself, already filled in.

4 Forward
This duplicates any email message you have received in a message window, but leaves the

190 **Sending Emails**

200 **Receiving Emails**

178 **Launching Outlook Express**

CUSTOMIZING THE TOOLBAR

To customize the toolbar click on the **View** menu, then on **Layout**, and then click **Customize Toolbar**. Toolbar buttons can be removed, or further ones can be added from the list of available buttons. The order of the buttons on the toolbar can be changed by clicking on the **Move up** or **Move down** buttons. The **Text Options** pull-down menu allows you to change the text, and the size of the icons can be changed by dropping down the **Icon Options** menu.

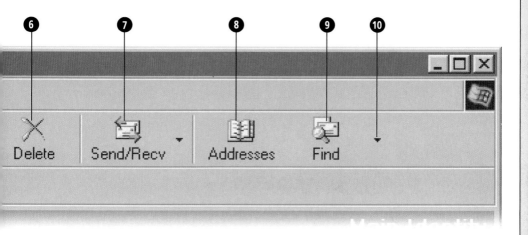

THE TOOLBAR BUTTONS

address field blank for you to forward the contents to someone else by typing a new address.

⑤ Print

Clicking this button prints a copy of the email message that you have selected.

⑥ Delete

Deletes the email message you have selected in the Message List.

⑦ Send/Receive

This sends any messages in the Outbox and checks for new mail.

⑧ Addresses

This opens the Address Book belonging to the current user and shows names and addresses, which can be selected.

⑨ Find

Opens a search dialog box so

that you can search for messages by criteria such as sender and recipient.

⑩ More Find Options

*Clicking on the arrow to the right of the **Find** button drops down a menu containing further search options including searching for a particular sequence of words.*

PERSONALIZING THE OUTLOOK EXPRESS WINDOW

Once you have become familiar with Outlook Express and know which features you find most useful, you may want to personalize the main window so that it shows only those panels and toolbars that you use on a day-to-day basis.

1 BEGINNING WITH THE VIEW MENU

This can be done from the **View** menu by following these instructions.

● Click the mouse on the **View** menu.

● Choose **Layout** from the drop-down menu that appears. The **Window Layout Properties** dialog box now opens.

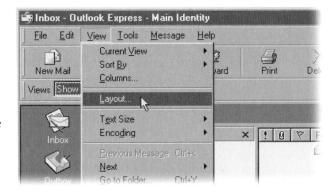

2 WINDOW LAYOUT PROPERTIES

Click the mouse in the various check boxes, in such a way that there are check marks beside all the items that you want to be displayed in the main window. Remove the check marks from items you do not want displayed.

● Click the **OK** button to save your new settings.

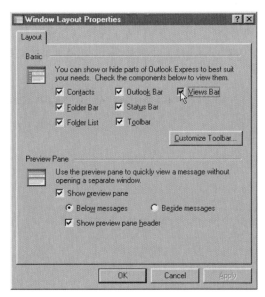

ONLINE AND OFFLINE WORKING

If you live in a country where you have to pay telephone charges each time you access the internet, or if your service provider charges you according to how long you spend online (connected to the internet), it will pay you to master the art of online and offline working at an early stage. It is perfectly feasible to do most of your electronic communication offline – that is, without being connected to your service provider. Composing, reading, and replying to messages can all be done offline. The only time you actually need to be connected to your service provider is when you want to send or receive communications, and this can usually be done in a matter of seconds. This section shows you how to move between online and offline modes and how to set up Outlook Express to reduce online time.

LAUNCHING OUTLOOK EXPRESS IN OFFLINE MODE

● Launch the Outlook Express program ⬚, but do not connect to your service provider first.

● In the **Dial-up Connection** box, click the **Work Offline** button with the mouse. Outlook Express will now open but you will not be connected to the internet. You can now read and compose ⬚ any email messages you wish without clocking up online time.

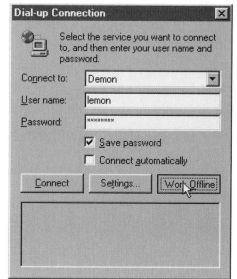

The Working Offline Icon

When you are working in Outlook Express, it is easy to check quickly whether or not you are offline by looking at the Status bar ⬚ at the bottom of the screen, where the **Working Offline** icon will appear.

GOING ONLINE

After you have finished
working offline and are
ready to send and receive
messages, you can go
online manually (see
below) or automatically
(see opposite).

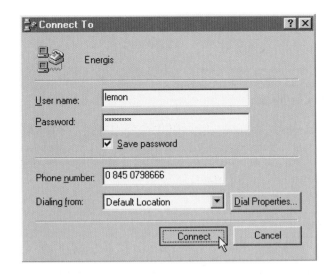

CONNECTING
MANUALLY

● Firstly connect to your
service provider in the
normal way.

● Now click on the **File**
icon in the Toolbar, and
from the pull-down menu
deselect **Work Offline**
(which should have a check
mark next to it) by clicking
it with the mouse. You are
now in online mode.

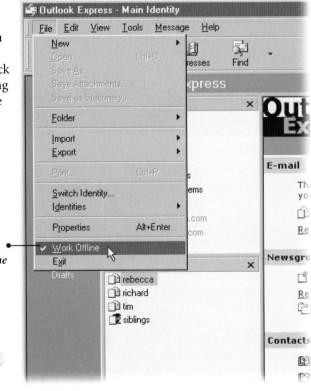

Deselecting ●———
Work Offline

CONNECTING AUTOMATICALLY

Click on the **Send/Recv** button. This will prompt you to connect to your service provider.

● Click **Yes**, and then click **Connect** (unless your connection is automatic, in which case omit this step). Once the connection is made, messages in the Outbox will be sent immediately. Outlook Express also checks for new email messages and downloads them to your Inbox .

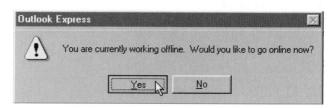

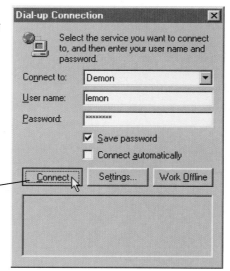

Connecting to the service provider

GOING OFFLINE

If you are online and you have some work that you can do offline, you can simply disconnect from your service provider in the usual way. However, there is an alternative.

Pull down the **File** menu and click on **Work Offline**. The menu closes and your online connection is broken automatically leaving the program running.

---

198 Sending later

200 Checking for Mail

CONFIGURING EXPRESS TO REDUCE ONLINE TIME

● You can set up Outlook Express so that it will automatically disconnect from your service provider after performing activities such as sending and receiving mail. This ensures that online time is kept to a minimum. To do this:

● Click on **Tools** in the Menu bar and then choose **Options**. The **Options** dialog box opens.

● Click on the **Connection** tab to bring it to the front and click in the check box next to **Hang up after sending and receiving**.

● Click the **OK** button to close the **Options** dialog box. Outlook Express now automatically disconnects from the internet after sending or receiving your email messages.

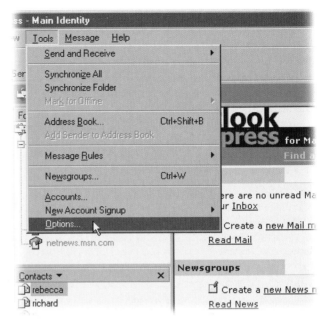

Check this box for automatic disconnection after sending and receiving

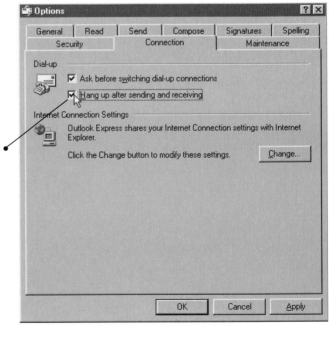

KEYBOARD SHORTCUTS

Throughout this book you will be shown how to carry out tasks in Outlook Express by using the Toolbar and the drop-down menus. However, many of the tasks can be accomplished using keyboard shortcuts. Unless you are used to using shortcuts in other programs, these keystroke combinations may seem clumsy at first, but you will soon find that they are quick and easy to use.

Select all messages .... Ctrl+A
Print selected message .... Ctrl+P
Send and receive mail .... Ctrl+M
Delete a mail message .... Del or Ctrl+D
Open or post a new message .... Ctrl+N
Open the Address Book .... Ctrl+⇧ Shift+B
Reply to the message author .... Ctrl+R
Forward a message .... Ctrl+F
Go to your Inbox .... Ctrl+I
Go to the next message in the list .... Ctrl+>
Go to the previous message in the list .... Ctrl+< or Ctrl+⇧ Shift+<
View properties of a selected message .... Alt+Enter↵
Go to next unread mail message .... Ctrl+U
Open a selected message .... Ctrl+O or Enter↵
Mark a message as read .... Ctrl+Enter↵
Move between Folders list, message list,
preview pane, and Contacts list .... Tab↹
Close a message .... Esc
Find text F3
Find a message .... Ctrl+⇧ Shift+F
Switch among Edit, Source, and Preview tabs .... Ctrl+Tab↹
Check spelling F7
Insert signature .... Ctrl+⇧ Shift+S
Send (post) a message .... Ctrl+Enter↵ or Alt+S

SENDING EMAILS

Composing and sending email messages is a simple process that uses basic word-processing skills, and is probably one of the first activities you will want to try. This chapter shows you how.

THE MESSAGE WINDOW

Email messages are composed in the Message Window, which is accessed by clicking the **New Mail** button on the toolbar ⬚. An email message is made up of several parts. The message "header" contains the sender, the recipient(s), and the subject of the message. The message "body" contains the message itself. A message may also contain other elements such as file attachments ⬚. These pages show the message window and how to use it to compose an email.

THE MESSAGE WINDOW

❶ The To: field
This contains the email address of the recipient of the message. Every message contains the address.

❷ The Cc: field
This contains the email addresses of people to whom you would like to send "carbon copies" of the message.

❸ The Subject: field
This contains the subject of the message. Filling in the subject is optional, but it is good practice to use a subject so that people can tell at a glance what your message is about.

❹ Message Body
This is where you type the text of the message. It acts as a normal word-processing window.

❺ Toolbar
This provides access to the main activities you will want to carry out when typing a message. There are buttons for editing text (cut, copy, and paste); for checking spelling; and for sending and prioritizing the message when it is finished.

❻ Formatting Toolbar
This offers some of the standard word-processing features to enable you to align text, choose the font and style, manage paragraphs, and add bullet points. Formatting can only be applied to text that has been selected (by clicking and dragging the mouse). Not all email programs have the sophisticated word-processing features that Outlook Express contains. If you do not know which program the addressee has on their computer, it is advisable not to add complex formatting to your email message because their email program may not have the facilities to display it.

⬚ 182 | The Toolbar

⬚ 193 | Adding attachments

COMPOSING OFFLINE

You may be composing a message offline to be sent later, and possibly to reduce phone bills. When you save a message when working offline, the message is saved to the Outbox. When you have finished the message and go online, the message is sent automatically from the Outbox.

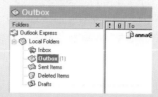

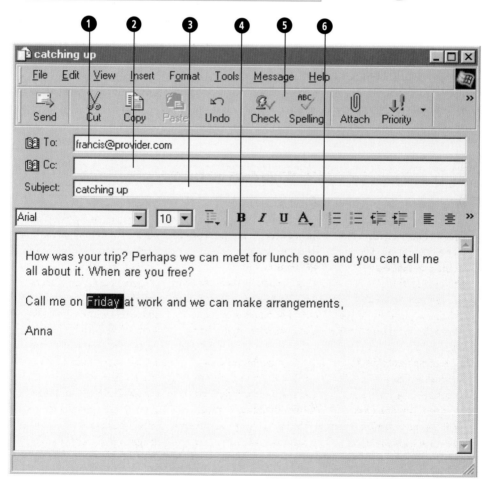

COMPOSING A MESSAGE

Composing a message can involve a number of different steps, which depend, for example, on whether you wish to include extra files, how many recipients there are, or whether you intend to send the message immediately. This section shows the basic process of composing an email and refers you to other sections where you will find information on how to carry out the other options.

COMPOSING A NEW MESSAGE

● Select a mail folder, such as the **Inbox** or **Outbox**, by clicking it in the **Folder** list or **Folder** bar.

● Click the **New Mail** button on the toolbar. This opens a new Outlook Express message window.

● Click the mouse in the message body area of the window and type the text of your message.

● Address the message .

● Add any file attachments you want to send with the message.

● Send the message.

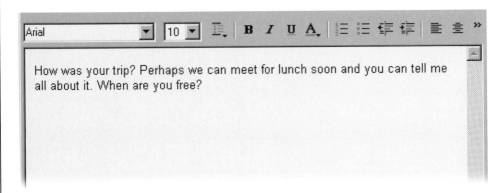

> How was your trip? Perhaps we can meet for lunch soon and you can tell me all about it. When are you free?

196 Addressing a Message

193 Adding attachments

198 Sending Messages
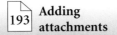

ADDING CONTACTS TO THE ADDRESS BOOK

Outlook Express uses the standard Windows Address Book to store contact details. While running Outlook Express, there are three ways to add an address.

ADDING FROM A MESSAGE

Open a message and click on **Tools** in the Menu bar. Click on **Add to Address Book** and choose **Sender** from the submenu. An Address Book **Properties** box opens showing the name and email address that have been taken from the message. Click on **OK** to add these details to the Address Book.

ADDING FROM THE INBOX

In the Inbox Message list, right-click on a message whose sender is to be added to the Address Book. Simply choose **Add Sender to Address Book** from the pop-up menu to add the address.

USING THE CONTACT PANEL

Click on the **Contacts** button in the Contact panel, and choose **New Contact** from the drop-down menu. A **Properties** box opens, click in the **E-Mail Address** field and type the email address. Click on **OK** to save the details.

WORKING WITH ATTACHMENTS AND FILES

As well as the text of an email message, you can also send files. These files are "attached" to your message. Attachments can include word-processing documents, images, sound or video files, and even computer programs. When you send an attachment, your computer copies the file and sends it with the message – the original stays on your computer. You can send more than one file with a message. Alternatively, you can insert the contents of the file into the message body itself. To add an attachment or insert the contents of a file into a message, follow these steps.

ADDING ATTACHMENTS

● With a message window 🗋 open, click on the **Attach** button on the toolbar.

● In the **Insert Attachment** dialog box, which is now open, navigate to the file you want to attach by double-clicking folders to open them.

● Click on the file you wish to attach so that it becomes highlighted and then click the **Attach** button.

● A new field appears in the mail header showing the name of the file(s) you have just attached.

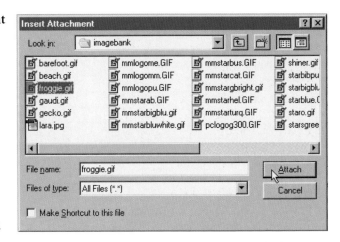

Attached picture file ●

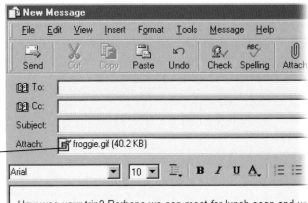

CHECK THE FILE SIZE AND TYPE

Sending large files as attachments increases the size of the message and the length of time it takes to download. Files over 500KB can take a significant time to download, particularly on a slow modem, so always check the size of a file you want to send. To do this, right-click the mouse on the file and select **Properties** from the pop-up menu. If you are attaching or inserting image files, try to use GIF or JPEG format files. These are the standard types of format for images on the internet and nearly everyone can open them. They have a smaller file size than many other file formats.

INSERTING FILES

● To insert a file within the message, click in the message where you would like to insert the file and click on **Insert** in the Menu bar to select the desired file type, such as **Picture**.

● In the **Picture** dialog box, navigate to the file you want to insert and click so that it becomes highlighted, then click the **Open** button.

● You will see the contents of the file appear in the message body.

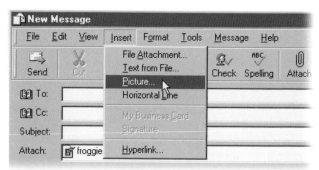

The name of the selected picture file ●

Picture file inserted ●
into the email

ADDRESSING A MESSAGE

When you have composed a message and added any attachments, the final step before sending it is to add the email address of the recipient(s). Unlike ordinary letters, you can send a single electronic message simultaneously to as many people as you want by simply including all their email addresses in the address field. It is important when addressing a message to make sure that you spell and punctuate the address exactly. If any extra characters or spaces creep in, the message will not be delivered to its destination because the computer will not understand the address. This page shows how to address messages manually, by typing. It is also possible to address messages directly from the Address Book, but before you can do that you need to create records for your email contacts.

1 TYPING THE ADDRESS

● Position the mouse pointer in the Address field of the message window.
● Type the recipient's email address. There should be no spaces in the address, and follow capitalization and punctuation exactly.

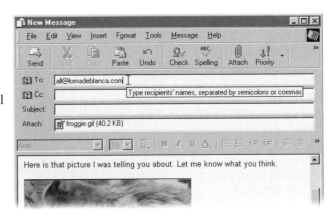

2 USING CARBON COPIES

● You can send a "carbon copy" of an email to one or more people at the same time as you send the original message by using the Cc: field in the message header. To send someone a carbon copy, click in the Cc: field and then type their email address.

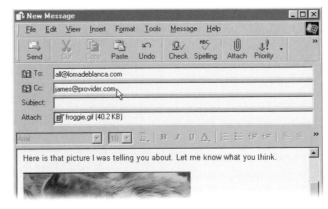

192 Composing a new message

3 MULTIPLE RECIPIENTS

If you wish to include more than one email address in the address or the Cc: field, you can do so easily:

● Click the mouse in the address or Cc: field.

● Type the first email address, taking care to replicate exactly the punctuation and spelling.

● Type a semicolon or a comma, then a space, and then the next email address. Repeat this step for each new address that you want to include.

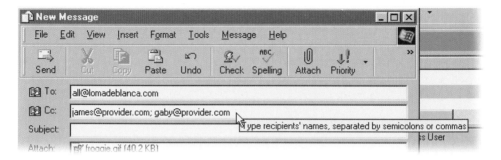

SAVING A DRAFT

You can stop composing a message and save it to be completed at a later date in the same way that you can save any other computer file. Saved messages are known as "drafts."

● In the Message window click on **File** and choose **Save**.

● Your message is saved as a draft in the **Drafts** folder.

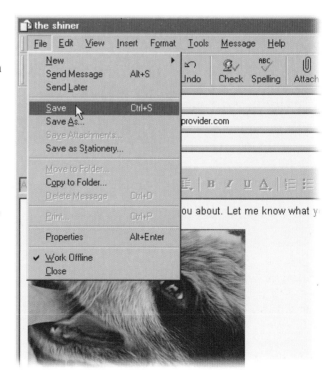

SENDING MESSAGES

Outlook Express offers several options when sending: you can send a message at once or send it later. For example, you can use **Send Options** to keep copies of messages, or to record automatically the addresses of people who write to you.

1 THE MESSAGE WINDOW

● To send a message you have finished composing, click the **Send** button on the toolbar. If you are online, it will be sent immediately. If you are offline, the message will be automatically stored in the Outbox ready for sending when you go online.

2 SENDING LATER

If you have finished a message, but do not want to send it immediately, you can store it to be sent later.
● Click on **File** in the Menu bar and select **Send Later**. The message is saved in the Outbox ready for sending when you go online to send your messages.

3 SENDING FROM MAIN WINDOW

● Click the **Send/Recv** button on the main toolbar ⬏. You are prompted to connect to your service provider. All messages that are in the Outbox are sent as soon as the connection has been made.

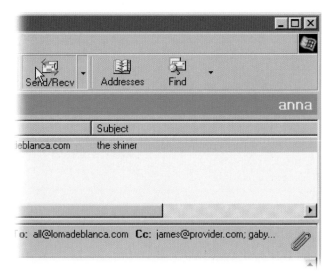

4 SETTING THE SEND OPTIONS

There are many choices you can make about how Outlook handles your email. In the **Send Options** dialog box you can personalize the settings. To select the available options:

● Open the **Send Options** dialog box by clicking on **Tools** in the Menu bar and choosing **Options**.

● Click on the **Send** tab to bring it to the front. A list of sending options appears.

● Choose your preferred options by clicking in the check boxes so that there is a check mark next to the options you want to be active. Click the **OK** button to save your options.

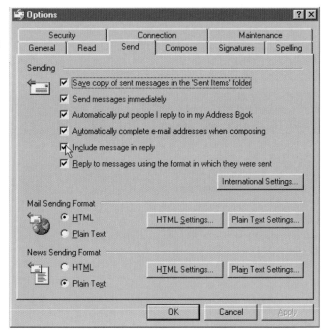

182 **The Toolbar**

RECEIVING EMAILS

Once you're familiar with Outlook Express and have sent your first emails, you will be eager to receive replies. This chapter tells you about receiving and managing incoming messages.

CHECKING FOR MAIL

When you launch 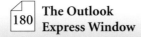 Outlook Express and go online, among the first tasks the program performs is checking your mail server for incoming mail and downloading new messages into your Inbox so that you can read them. However, you can check for new mail at any time after that. This page shows you how to check for and retrieve new messages manually, and how to configure Outlook Express to do this automatically. There are several methods that you can use to check for new mail. To try them out, first open the **Inbox** by clicking the **Inbox** button or folder in either the Outlook bar or the **Folders** list. When you want to receive mail you will need to go online. If you try to collect mail while offline, you will be prompted to connect to your service provider.

USING THE MENU

● Click on the **Tools** in the Menu bar and choose **Send and Receive**. From the submenu that appears, choose either **Send and Receive All** or **Receive All**, depending on whether or not you wish to send messages at the same time as checking for new ones.

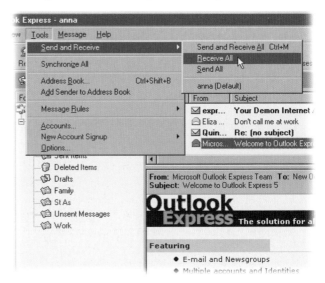

FROM THE TOOLBAR

● On the main toolbar, click the down arrow on the right-hand side of the Send/Recv button. A drop-down menu appears listing several receive options. Choose the desired option by clicking on it.

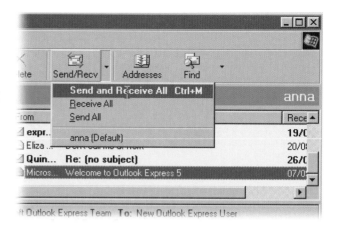

USING THE SEND/ RECV BUTTON

● Click the Send/Recv button on the main toolbar. New messages appear in the message list and any mail waiting in your outbox is sent.

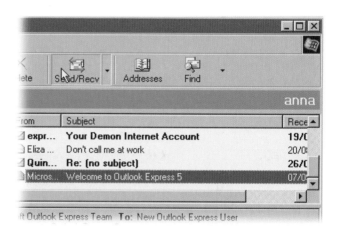

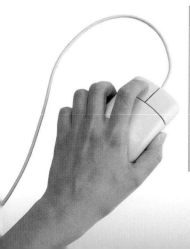

MESSAGE REQUEST

After performing any of the above methods for receiving new messages, Outlook Express will contact your mail server and request all the messages that are waiting in your mailbox. If there are messages waiting, Outlook Express will transfer them to your computer and store them in the **Inbox** folder; if there are no new messages Outlook Express will simply tell you so.

AUTOMATIC MAIL CHECKING

If you spend long periods of time online – surfing the web, for example – you may want to configure Outlook Express to check automatically for incoming messages at periodic intervals. You can also ask it to alert you when you have new mail, by a dialog box or sound, for example. You can do this in the Outlook Express **Options**. These facilities will only operate when Outlook Express is running.

SETTING UP MAIL OPTIONS

● Click **Tools** on the Main menu and choose **Options**.
● In the **Options** dialog box, click on the **General** tab to bring it to the front. Move down to the **Send/Receive Messages** section and click in the check boxes to place a check mark against the options that you want to be active.
● To set how often Outlook Express checks the server for new mail, click on the up or down arrows in the minutes window until the required interval is shown.
● Click the **OK** button to finish and save the options.

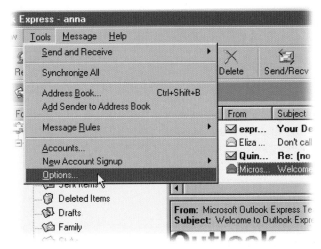

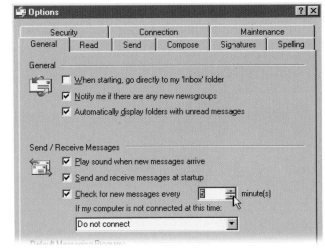

READING INCOMING MESSAGES

All your incoming email arrives by default in a message folder called the **Inbox**. The **Inbox** can be accessed either from the Outlook bar or the **Folders** list. It stores and lists all your incoming messages. You may notice that some messages in the Inbox appear in a bold typeface. These are new, or "unread," messages. When you want to read these messages all you have to do is to click the **Inbox** folder, then select the message you want to read in the message list. As usual, there are several ways in which you can read your incoming mail. To try them out, first open the **Inbox** by clicking on the **Inbox** icon on the Outlook bar.

1 OPENING A MESSAGE

● In the Inbox message list, choose which message you want to read and then double-click the message.

● Alternatively, you can select the message by clicking it once with the mouse, and then press the [Enter ←] key to open the message. A message window opens displaying the contents of the message. If the message is too long to fit in the window, use the scroll bars at the side to scroll down through the text.

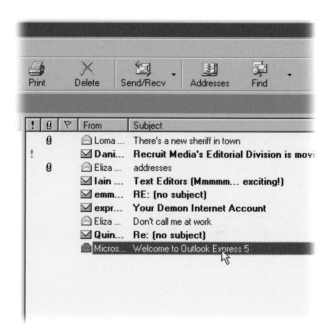

THE NEW MAIL ICON

It is easy to tell when new messages arrive because a **New Mail** icon appears on the Windows taskbar. This has the appearance of an envelope. To be able to view the messages, you must go to your Inbox in the main Outlook Express window ⌐.

180 The Outlook Express Window

2 READING OTHER MESSAGES

● If you have several new messages, you can read them all from the same message window using the **Next** and **Previous** buttons. Each time you click one of these buttons, the contents of the message window will change to show the next or previous message in the Message List.

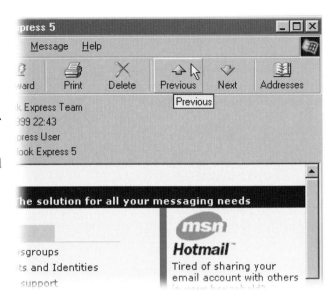

3 READING IN THE PREVIEW PANEL

If you have the Preview panel ☐ visible in the Outlook Express window ☐, you can read the contents of your messages without opening a message window at all. Click on the message you want to read in the Message List to display its contents in the Preview panel. You can move up and down through the Message List by using the cursor keys on the keyboard to read successive messages.

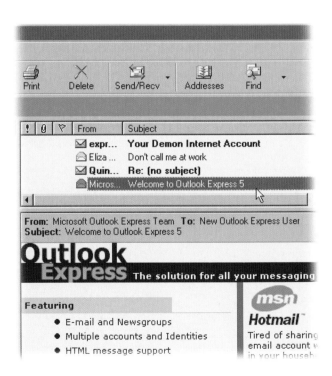

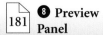

181 **❽ Preview Panel**

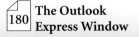

180 **The Outlook Express Window**

READ AND UNREAD MESSAGES

New or unread messages are displayed in bold. Once you have read them they are listed in a regular typeface. There may be occasions when you would like a message to remain in bold – to remind you to act on it, for example. Or, you may want to mark an unread message as "read" – to ignore it, for example.

Outlook enables you to change the status of read and unread messages manually. To do this, right-click the mouse on the message and choose **Mark as Read** or **Mark as Unread** from the pop-up menu that appears. You can also find these commands as options in the **Edit** menu.

RESPONDING TO MESSAGES

There are several ways in which you may wish to respond to incoming email. You may want to reply to the sender directly, to all the recipients of the message, or to forward the message on to someone else, perhaps including a brief note of your own. You may want to print the message, or you may not want to respond at all, but just move the message to a new folder so that you can keep it for reference. Outlook provides for all of these eventualities. Many of these activities can be carried out from the message window. To practice them, first open the message.

1 REPLYING TO THE SENDER

● To reply to the sender, click the **Reply** button on the toolbar. A message window opens with the contents of the sender's message included, and his or her email address inserted in the **To:** field. Type your response and send it in the normal way.

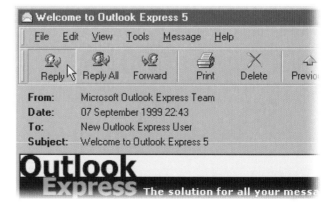

2 REPLYING TO ALL

● To reply to the sender of the message as well as all the other people to whom the message was circulated, click the **Reply to All** button on the toolbar. A message window will open with the contents of the sender's message included, and all the recipients' addresses listed in the address fields.

● Compose your response and then send it in the normal way.

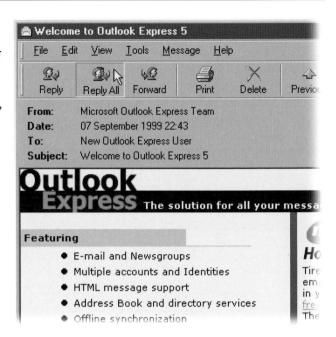

3 FORWARDING MESSAGES

● To forward a message to one or more people, click the **Forward** button on the toolbar. A message window will open with the contents of the sender's message included, but the address field will be blank.

● If you want to add remarks of your own, click the mouse at the top of the typing area and type your message in that area.

● Address the message to the recipients and send it in the usual way ⌐.

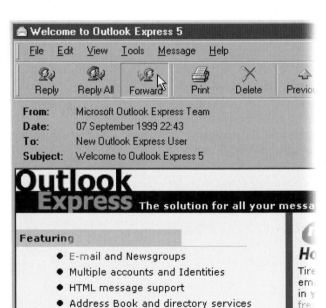

196 Typing the address

198 Sending Messages

4 PRINTING THE MESSAGE

● To print the message, click the **Print** button on the toolbar. If the **Print Properties** dialog box appears, choose from the print options and then click the **OK** button.

VIEWING ATTACHMENTS

Just as you can send files to other people as attachments 🗋, you can also receive files with an email. A message that carries an attachment is displayed in the Message List 🗋 with a paper clip icon next to it. You could be sent all sorts of files as attachments: image files, text files, multimedia files, or computer programs. When you receive an attachment you have two choices: to save it as a file or to open it. To do either, first open the message in a message window 🗋. All the attachments for that particular message are listed in the Attach field in the message header.

1 SELECTING ATTACHMENTS

● In the Message window, click on **File** in the Main menu and choose **Save Attachments**. A list of the attachments will appear in the **Save Attachments** dialog box.

● If there is more than one attachment, click the **Select All** button to select save the attached files.

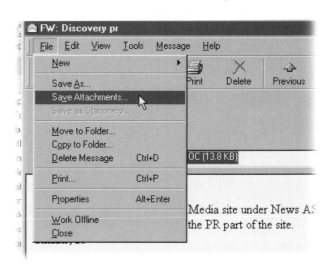

---

2 SAVING ATTACHMENTS

● Click the **Browse** button with the mouse and navigate to the folder where you want to save the file(s), then click the **OK** button in the **Browse for Folder** box.

● Click the **Save** button in the **Save Attachments** dialog box to complete the process. The attachment is now saved in the folder that you selected.

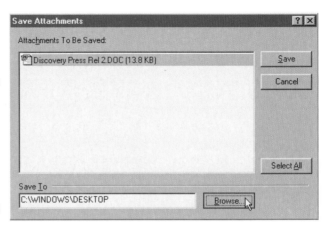

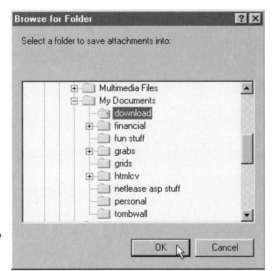

VIRUS CHECKERS

It is a wise precaution to check any attachments that you are sent for viruses before opening them. Many malicious viruses are distributed by email, often attaching themselves to messages without your knowledge. Be particularly wary of program files (these have a .exe file extension) that you are not expecting to receive. If you are in any doubt about the source of the file and its contents, use a virus checking program. There are many virus checking programs on the internet that you can download without charge.

3 OPENING ATTACHMENTS

• To open an attachment directly from the message window, double-click the mouse on the file icon in the Attach field in the message header. The file will then open using the software needed to view it. If the computer does not have the necessary software an error message will appear telling you that the computer does not recognize the file or does not have the required program to open it.

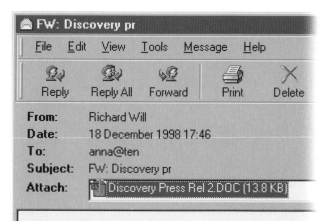

FW: Discovery pr

File   Edit   View   Tools   Message   Help

Reply   Reply All   Forward   Print   Delete

From: Richard Will
Date: 18 December 1998 17:46
To: anna@ten
Subject: FW: Discovery pr
Attach: Discovery Press Rel 2.DOC (13.8 KB)

Dear Anna,
Please could you put this on the Media site und
with the other Press Releases in the PR part of
Thanks, R.

FILE EXTENSIONS

When you want to open an attachment (even if you have saved it first), you will require the software that is capable of handling that particular type of file.

Usually it is possible to tell what type of file an attachment is from its extension. Some of the common file types you are likely to encounter are listed here.

File Extension	File Type	Software Required
.txt	Text document	Notepad, Word
.zip	Compressed file	Winzip
.xls	Spreadsheet	Excel
.exe	Program file	Runs itself
.doc	Word text file	Word
.pdf	Portable document file	Acrobat Reader
.jpg	JPEG image file	Photoshop, Paint Shop Pro
.gif	GIF image file	Explorer, Navigator
.tif	Tagged Image File	Photoshop, Paint Shop Pro
.psd	Photoshop image file	Photoshop, Paint Shop Pro

MANAGING YOUR EMAIL MESSAGES

There is more to email than just receiving and reading, and composing and sending messages. If you become an active email correspondent, before long your **Inbox** (and **Sent Messages** folder) will become so full as to be overflowing. Many people find it useful to create new mail folders into which they can move messages to be kept. Messages that you do not want have to be deleted on a regular basis to save valuable space on the hard disk. This section shows how to perform the basic activities that will help you manage your email messages effectively.

1 DELETING MESSAGES

To delete a message from the message list, click on the message file and then press the [Del] key on the keyboard or the Delete button on the toolbar. The message is removed from the message list and transferred to the Deleted Items folder.

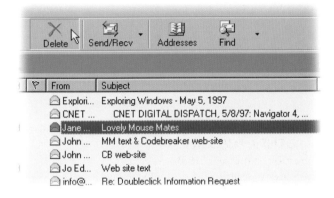

2 CREATING A NEW FOLDER

● Position the mouse on one of the folders in the **Folders** list ⌐ and right-click the mouse once. From the pop-up menu choose **New Folder**. The **Create Folder** dialog box opens.

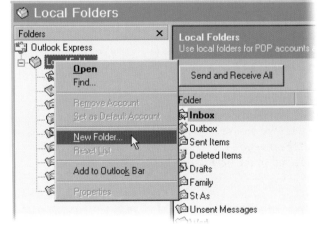

❹ **Folders List**

- Click the mouse in the **Folder Name** field and type the name of the folder.
- In the **Folders** list below click the mouse on the folder in which you would like to create the new folder. The folder becomes highlighted.
- Click the **OK** button to create the folder. The new folder will now appear in the **Folders** list.

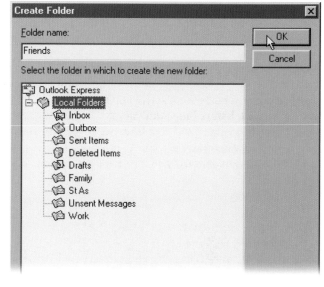

3 MOVING TO OTHER FOLDERS

- To move a message from one folder to another, ensure that the **Folders** list and the Message window are visible.
- Place the mouse pointer over the message you want to move and hold down the mouse button.
- Drag the mouse pointer until it is over the folder into which you would like to move the message. Release the mouse button and the message is relocated in the new folder.

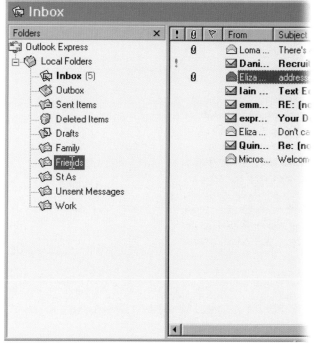

4 DELETING FOLDERS

To delete a folder from the **Folders** list:

● Click the mouse on the folder you want to delete so that it becomes highlighted.

● Press the [Del] key or the **Delete** button on the toolbar to delete the folder.

● Confirm the operation by clicking the **Yes** button. The folder is removed from the **Folders** list.

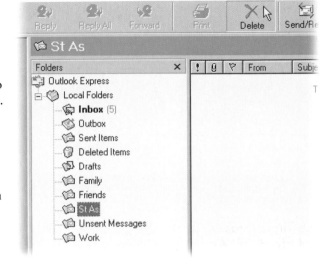

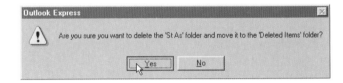

5 SAVING MESSAGES AS FILES

To save an email as a file that you can access from programs other than Outlook Express, open the message in a Message Window ⌐ and click the mouse on the **File** menu. Select **Save As** from the drop-down menu and then navigate to the folder where you want to save the file.

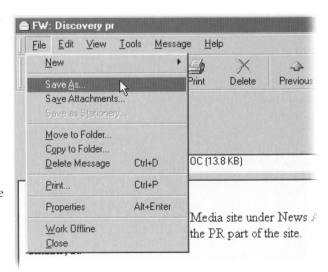

Media site under News /
the PR part of the site.

- Type the name of the file in the **File name** field and then click the **Save** button with the mouse to finish the process.

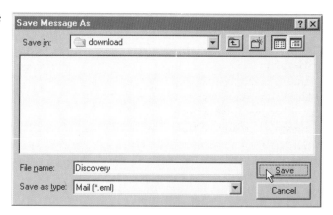

READING MESSAGES BY USING VIEWS

You can preselect how your messages are displayed.

- Click on **View** in the Menu bar and choose **Current View**. A submenu opens with several views. The main views have the following effect:
- **Show all messages:** All messages in one of your folders are displayed.
- **Hide read messages:** This view hides messages once you've read them.
- **Hide read or ignored messages:** This view hides read messages and those you have told Outlook Express to ignore.

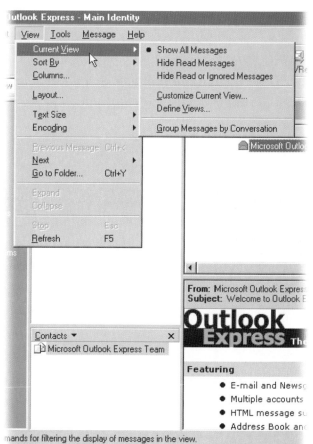

BUILDING
A WEBSITE

BUILDING A WEBSITE is an easy-to-follow guide to Microsoft's website-building program, FrontPage 2000. This section is for anyone who has little or no experience with FrontPage 2000. FrontPage 2000's features, from creating a new site, through working with text and images, creating links, and using table and forms, to publishing your completed website on the web, are presented in separate chapters to allow easy understanding of their functions and how to carry them out.

MICROSOFT FRONTPAGE

FrontPage 2000 is a comprehensive website creation and management tool. Its flexibility makes it ideal for creating websites from personal home pages to corporate internet sites.

WHAT CAN FRONTPAGE DO?

Creating the pages that make up a website used to be the exclusive preserve of computer programmers with a deep and comprehensive knowledge of the HTML programming language, which is used to create web pages. With FrontPage 2000, it is no longer necessary to know HTML. FrontPage 2000 carries out the programming for you in the background, allowing you to concentrate on the essential features in your web pages such as design, feel, and functionality. The program is easy to learn and use because as well as containing advanced authoring tools, it also contains simple controls that you can begin to use almost immediately. FrontPage 2000 takes you through every aspect of creating web pages from opening a blank screen to finally publishing your site on the web.

WHAT IS FRONTPAGE?

FrontPage 2000 is essentially an editing tool, just like a word-processing program such as Microsoft Word. Whereas Word is used to create text and graphics that are eventually printed out on hard copy, FrontPage 2000 allows you to produce text and graphics easily and creatively, which will eventually appear on the World Wide Web.

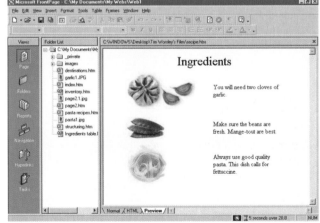

LAUNCHING FRONTPAGE

FrontPage 2000 is a powerful program that is probably different from any other kind of software that you've used.

However, FrontPage has many familiar features, and can be launched from the desktop just like any other program.

1 LAUNCHING VIA THE START MENU

● Place the mouse cursor over the **Start** button in the Taskbar and click. Move the cursor up the menu to **Programs**. A submenu appears on screen.

● Move the cursor across to **Microsoft FrontPage** and click the left mouse button.

● The FrontPage window opens on screen ☐.

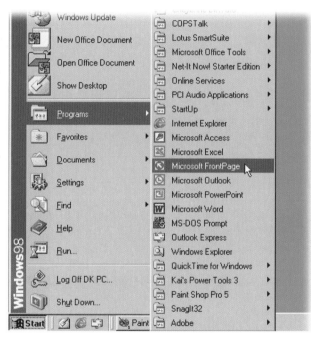

2 LAUNCHING FRONTPAGE VIA A SHORTCUT

● You may already have a shortcut to FrontPage on your desktop. Double-click the icon.

● The FrontPage window opens on screen ☐.

218 The FrontPage Window

THE FRONTPAGE WINDOW

The window that opens when you launch FrontPage 2000 has a style and layout that will be familiar to you if you've used other Microsoft Office 2000 applications. The features present in the window are designed around the actions that you carry out to create a website, and several view options to see what you've created.

THE FRONTPAGE WINDOW

1 The Views bar
To select the view options
2 Title bar
3 Menu bar
All the options in menus
4 Standard toolbar
Buttons for frequent actions
5 View title bar
Title of what is viewed
6 Workspace area
Where the web is built
7 Formatting toolbar
Options for style and layout
8 Close view button
Closes the contents of display
9 Insertion point
Shows where typing appears
10 Page view
To view current web page
11 Folders view
To organize files and folders
12 Reports view
Shows status of files/links
13 Navigation view
Shows navigation structure
14 Hyperlinks view
Displays web's hyperlinks ⌐

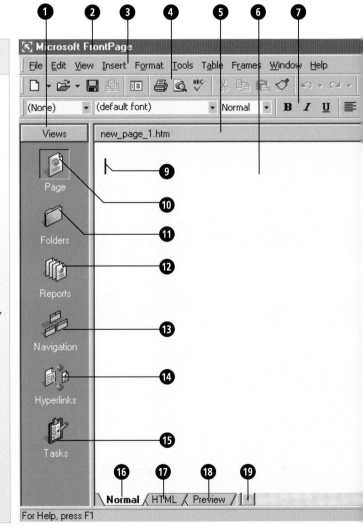

242 Creating Links

SMALL ICONS?

The **Views** bar is shown by default to the left of the workspace and allows you to switch quickly between views. If you prefer, you can use small icons in the **Views** bar by right-clicking on the bar and selecting **Small Icons** from the menu that opens.

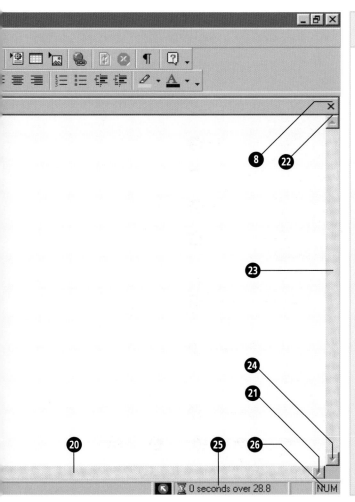

THE FRONTPAGE WINDOW

⑮ Tasks view
Shows outstanding tasks
⑯ Normal view tab
Web page is created here ⌐
⑰ HTML code tab
HTML code is shown here
⑱ Preview tab
Shows page in browser view
⑲ Scroll left arrow
Shows left side of page
⑳ Scroll bar
Used to move across page
㉑ Scroll right arrow
Shows right side of page
㉒ Scroll up arrow
Shows top of page
㉓ Vertical scroll bar
Used to show all the page
㉔ Scroll down arrow
To show end of page
㉕ Download time
Time taken for page to download ⌐
㉖ NUM lock
Shows that numeric keypad at right of keyboard is on

┌─┐
│224│ **Creating a Page**
└─┘

┌─┐
│234│ **A word about download times**
└─┘

THE FRONTPAGE TOOLBARS

FrontPage is part of the suite of programs that comprise the Microsoft Office 2000 suite. And as such its toolbars follow closely the style and layout of the other programs in the suite. You will notice a strong similarity to the toolbars that are part of Word because both Word and FrontPage feature powerful editing tools. Other toolbars are available for display in the FrontPage window, and if you want to customize these, follow the sequence of steps described opposite.

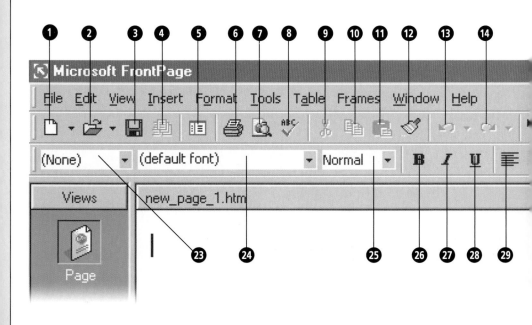

THE FRONTPAGE TOOLBARS

1. New page
2. Open file/folder
3. Save
4. Publish website
5. Folder list
6. Print
7. Preview in browser
8. Spelling checker
9. Cut
10. Copy
11. Paste
12. Format painter
13. Undo action(s)
14. Redo action(s)
15. Insert component
16. Insert table
17. Insert picture from file
18. Hyperlink
19. Refresh screen
20. Stop link or loading
21. Show formatting marks
22. Help
23. Style selector
24. Font selector

CUSTOMIZING A TOOLBAR

You can select which toolbars to see and their contents. Click **Tools** in the Menu bar and select **Customize**. The **Customize** dialog box opens. Click on the **Toolbars** tab to see the list of ten available toolbars.

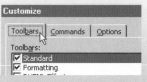

ScreenTips

You don't have to memorize what each button does. Just roll the mouse cursor over a button, wait one second, and a box appears and gives the button's name.

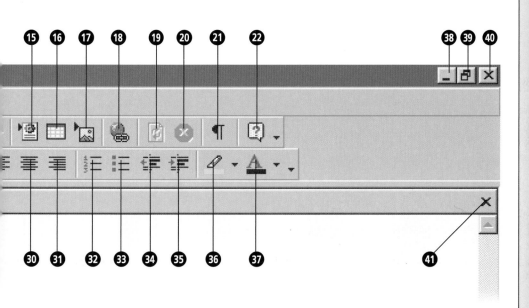

THE FRONTPAGE TOOLBARS

- ㉕ Font size selector
- ㉖ Bold
- ㉗ Italic
- ㉘ Underline
- ㉙ Align left
- ㉚ Center
- ㉛ Align right
- ㉜ Numbering list
- ㉝ Bulleted list
- ㉞ Decrease indent
- ㉟ Increase indent
- ㊱ Highlight color
- ㊲ Text color
- ㊳ Minimize window
- ㊴ Restore window
- ㊵ Close FrontPage
- ㊶ Close web page

|229| **Aligning text**

|231| **Using Lists**

CREATING A NEW WEB

FrontPage removes all the hard labor from creating a new web. There's no need to learn a new programming language because FrontPage does all the programming for you in the background.

CREATING A FRONTPAGE WEB

FrontPage uses the concept of a "FrontPage Web" to organize the different files you create. This means you keep all the different elements of your website together in a group, which FrontPage calls a "web." Try to think of each FrontPage web as a unique project that can be worked on as a whole, rather than a series of individual files. You will use FrontPage to create your FrontPage web, which you can publish in its entirety. You can also make changes at any time and FrontPage will automatically update the rest of your site, keeping your site intact and error-free.

1 MAKING A NEW WEB
● To create a new FrontPage web, launch FrontPage, click on **File** in the menu bar, and choose **New** and then **Web** from the menus that drop down.

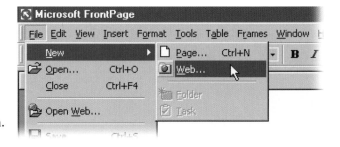

OTHER TYPES OF WEBSITES

FrontPage offers a variety of website types to choose from when creating a new web. We have chosen a One Page Web, but the other webs are fun to try out too. For example, choosing the **Corporate Presence** Wizard from the **New** dialog box launches a series of questions about you and your company, and creates the site structure based on your answers. You can customize the pages that have been created, and quickly have a good-looking website.

2 CHOOSING A WEB TYPE

● You are presented with the **New** dialog box offering a variety of different webs. For now, just highlight **One Page Web**. You also type in a location where the web is to be saved. In this example, the chosen path is: **C:\My Documents\ My Webs\Web1**, where **Web1** is the name given to the new web if this is the first web that has been created. Click on **OK** when you have entered these details.

● A new web is created containing an empty "home page" ready for you to customize, (a home page is the first page you arrive at when you visit a site).

The different types of web on offer

Type the desired location of the new web in this box ●

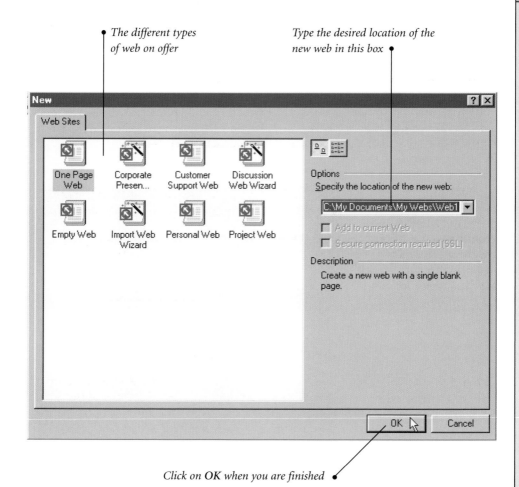

Click on OK when you are finished ●

CREATING A PAGE

So far you have created a One Page Web containing a single home page. This page is empty and is ready for you to start filling it with information, but before doing that it's important to know how to save the page and how to create new pages. You can see a list of the files in your web by using the **Folder List** area of the FrontPage environment (if you can't see it, choose **Folder List** from the **View** menu). The **Folder List** area is similar to the Windows Explorer feature of Windows. The two folders, **_private** and **images**, are created by FrontPage.

1 OPENING A PAGE

● Double-click on the file you want to open in the **Folder List**. In this case, double-click on **index.htm** (the default name of the home page).

● The page opens in Normal view in the main workspace area of the screen. Now position the cursor at the top of the page and type **Welcome to my home page!**.

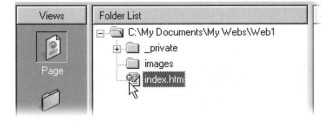

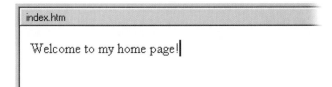

2 SAVING A PAGE

● Now that you have added some text to the page, you can save the changes you have made. Choose **Save** from the **File** menu (or click on the **Save** button on the Standard toolbar). The file is now saved.

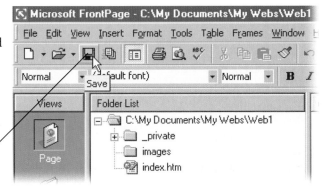

Save button ●

3 ADDING A PAGE

● To add new pages to your web, pull down the **File** menu, select **New** and then **Page**. A dialog box appears containing various types of pages. Just choose **Normal Page** and click **OK**.

● You can now add to this new page to your web, just as you did with the home page. When you decide to save this page, the **Save As** dialog box appears.

● Type **page2.htm** in the **File name:** box and then click the **Save** button. The page is now added to your web. You can add as many pages to your web as you want whenever you want.

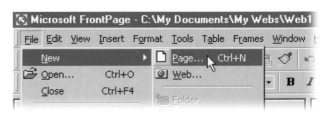

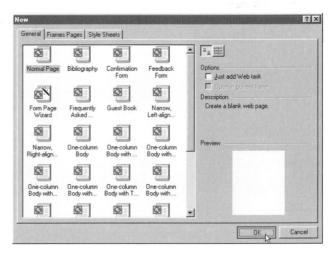

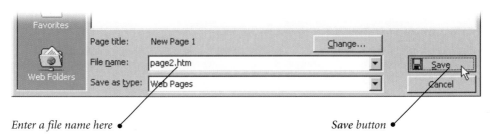

Enter a file name here ●   *Save button* ●

NAMING WEB PAGES

When choosing file names for your web pages, there are some points to keep in mind. Avoid putting letter spaces in the name, as this can cause problems on some web servers. Use the underscore symbol instead of a letter space, such as **new_page.htm**. Some web servers ☐ prefer all file names to be in lower-case letters, so it is common practice to use all lower-case file names as well. File names can be changed at any time.

270 **Publishing to a Web Server**

PAGE PROPERTIES

A web page has a set of **Page Properties**, such as a title or a background color. When FrontPage creates a new page it gives the page a set of default properties, but you can easily change these properties to suit your individual taste. Every web page should have a meaningful title because the title appears at the top of the web browser's window on a user's screen when they visit your website. You can also alter the color of the background of the page, and change the color of different parts of the text.

1 ACCESSING THE PAGE PROPERTIES

- Right-click on an empty section of your page and, from the pop-up menu that appears, choose **Page Properties** by left-clicking on it.

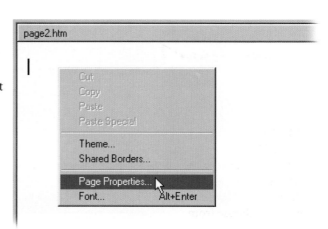

2 CHANGING THE PAGE TITLE

- Type a new title for your page in the Title box.

The Title box ●

3 CHANGING THE BACKGROUND

- To change the color of the background, click on the **Background** tab of the **Page Properties** dialog box.

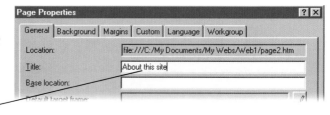

● Click on the arrow to the right of the **Background** box in the **Colors** section of the window to view the background colors.

● Click on the drop-down color palette to change your page's background color.

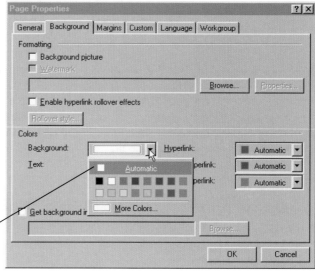

Background color drop-down palette ●

4 MORE COLORS

● If you need more colors than those on the initial palette, click on **More Colors**. Now choose from the wider selection.

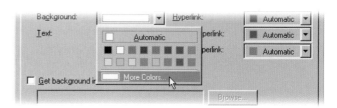

Click on a color to select it, and then click on OK ●

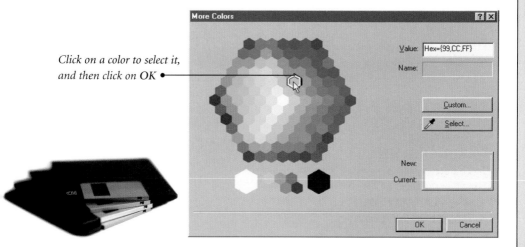

WORKING WITH TEXT

Text makes up the bulk of most websites. Learning how to create attractive text can make your website much easier to read and more enjoyable for your visitors.

ENTERING AND ALIGNING TEXT

Entering and aligning text using FrontPage is very similar to using a word processor, such as Microsoft Word. Text editing by using FrontPage should therefore be familiar to many people. The difference is that the text you type is formatted using HTML, which has a more limited range of styles than most word processors. However, you can still use most of the common techniques for text formatting, such as changing the alignment, creating headings, making text bold or underlined, and using different fonts and font sizes. Open the page called **index.htm** and begin the following exercises to build up your proficiency.

1 ENTERING TEXT

● As you have already seen, entering text into a web page is easy. Simply click on the text area of **index.htm** and type in your text.

Welcome to my home page!

This is some practice text that I'm typing in to see how manipulate text using Microsoft FrontPage 2000. No to press the Return key to start a new paragraph.

Here's my third paragraph.

2 ALIGNING TEXT

- Text can be aligned left, center, or right.
- To align some text, first highlight the paragraph you want to align, and then click on one of the alignment buttons on the formatting toolbar.
- To follow this example, highlight the paragraph **Welcome to my home page!**. Now click the **Center** alignment button to move the paragraph to the center of the page.

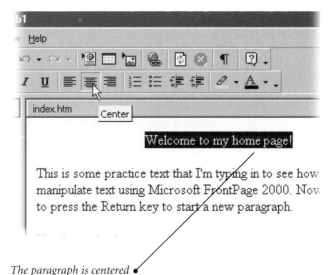

The paragraph is centered

STRUCTURING YOUR DOCUMENTS

HTML was designed to describe how a document is structured, and it contains a series of styles to help you do this. Each section of your document is given a tag that tells the browser what type of information is about to arrive. The most common tag is the paragraph tag. Each time you press [Enter ↵] when typing, FrontPage inserts an HTML paragraph tag. There are also many other types of tags, particularly Header tags, which can help you to structure your text.

1 ENTERING TEXT

- Create a page called **structuring.htm** and type in some text.
- Highlight the first line and click on the **Style selector** box at the left end of the Formatting toolbar ⌐.

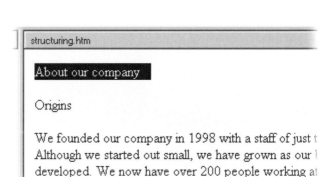

❷❸ **Style selector**

● Choose **Heading 1** from the list of pre-existing styles. The line changes to a larger font.

● Now choose the second line and do the same except this time choose **Heading 2**.

● You'll see that the line changes to a slightly smaller font than the **Heading 1** paragraph.

● Using the same method as before, make the fourth paragraph a **Heading 2**, and the fifth paragraph as **Heading 3**. Your page now has a logical structure.

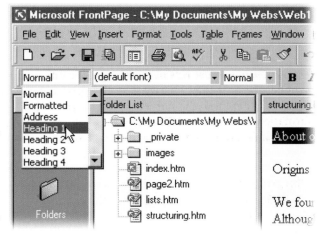

The first line now in the Heading 1 style •

The second line now in the Heading 2 style •

structuring.htm

About our company

Origins

We founded our company in 1998 with a staff of just t Although we started out small, we have grown as our developed. We now have over 200 people working at company headquarters.

THE BENEFITS OF STRUCTURING YOUR PAGE

There are good reasons to structure your pages by using different heading levels and paragraph types. For example, by defining one as an **H1** header, and the next as an **H2** header, a web browser knows to display the first heading in a larger size than the second. The actual way the browser displays the heading (such as using a specific font size) is determined by the browser itself. One browser might use a different font size from another, but the important thing is that the browser knows the correct proportion, or structure, of the way you want your page to be displayed on screen.

USING LISTS

Many people like to use lists in their documents because they are easy to read and can help emphasize important information. Fortunately, HTML has a built-in list function, and creating lists in FrontPage is very simple. We will concentrate on the two most widely used type of list, the bullet point list and the numbered list. Follow the instructions below to see how it's done.

1 NUMBERING LISTS

● Create a new page and call it **destinations.htm**. Insert the cursor at the place where you want your list to start.

● Suppose you are a travel agency and want a list of your most popular holiday destinations. Type in a series of cities as shown in the example, pressing `Enter ←` after each city.

● Now highlight the series of cities and click on the **Numbering list** button on the Formatting toolbar ▯. FrontPage creates a numbered list and adjusts the line spacing.

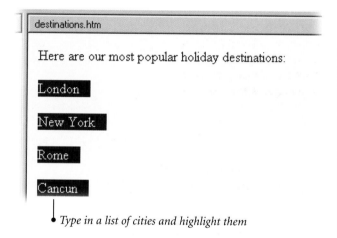

destinations.htm

Here are our most popular holiday destinations:

London

New York

Rome

Cancun

• *Type in a list of cities and highlight them*

destinations.htm

Here are our most popular holiday destinations:

1. London
2. New York
3. Rome
4. Cancun
5. Sydney

• *The list is now numbered*

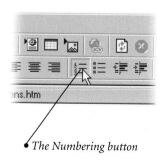

• *The Numbering button*

221 ❸ **Numbering list**

2 CREATING BULLET POINT LISTS

● Next, create a list showing the different types of ticket on offer. Type in the list as shown in the example.

● Highlight the list and click on the **Bulleted list** button on the Formatting toolbar. FrontPage creates a bullet point list.

We can offer flight tickets in the following classes:

First class

Business class

Economy class

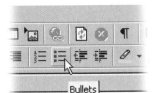

We can offer flight tickets in the following classes:

- First class
- Business class
- Economy class

FONTS AND STYLING

When you simply type text into a web page, you'll notice that it always appears in the same font. When a web browser reads your page it will display it using its default font. However, a variety of fonts, sizes, and styles is available to you. The browser reads the font instructions contained in the HTML code and displays your page in the way you intended. This can help give your page a more professional appearance.

1 CHANGING A FONT

● Open the home page called **index.htm** and highlight **Welcome to my home page!**.

● Click on the arrow to the right of the **Font selector** box to choose a font.

● Select **Arial**.

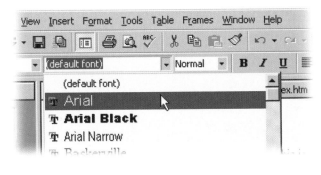

㉝ Bulleted list `221`

㉔ Font selector `220`

2 CHANGING THE FONT SIZE

- Next, click on the arrow next to the **Font size selector** box ⬚ on the Formatting toolbar to see a drop-down list of available font sizes.
- Choose 5 (**18pt**).
- The paragraph is now displayed in 18 point Arial, and stands out far better as a welcome to the page.

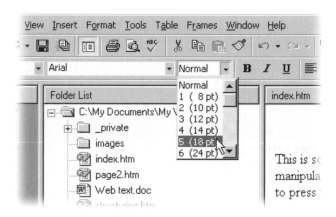

3 BOLD, ITALIC, AND UNDERLINE

- Using other text styles is easy. Just highlight a section of text (a word, a sentence, or a whole paragraph) and click on either the **Bold**, **Italic**, or **Underline** buttons.
- In this example, the word **third** is made bold.

*The **Bold** button* •

Here's my **third** parag⟶

STICK TO A FEW COMMON FONTS

Using too many fonts can make a page look messy, so stick to using one or two fonts per page. Also, you might choose a font that a visitor to your website might not have. The web browser substitutes the font with a close match, but the results are very unpredictable. It's best to stick to common fonts, such as Times New Roman, Arial, Helvetica, and Courier.

㉕ Font size selector

WORKING WITH IMAGES

Using images makes your web come alive, whether they are pictures of products for sale, photographs on your personal page, or graphical menus and buttons to enhance your pages.

WEB IMAGE FILE FORMATS

In order for images to be used on a website they must be saved in the correct file format. The two most widely used file formats are the GIF (Graphics Interchange Format) and JPEG (Joint Photographic Experts Group) formats. These are the best formats to use because almost all web browsers are able to display them. They are also useful because they are compressed file formats. This means that the image files are reduced in size when saved as a GIF or JPEG and visitors to your site are able to download the images faster. Without file compression, images take a long time before they are downloaded and displayed on screen. Potential visitors may decide that the wait is not worth it, and may leave your site.

A WORD ABOUT DOWNLOAD TIMES

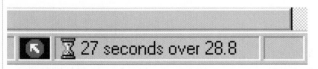

It's important to remember that adding multimedia files, such as pictures, animations, and videos, to a web page can increase its size very quickly and means that it will take longer for the page to appear when someone visits your site. This is because each image must be downloaded before it can be displayed on the page. The trick is to keep the overall download time for each page as small as you possibly can. FrontPage has a very useful feature that indicates the time it would take for each page to download using a typical 28.8K modem. This feature is displayed at the bottom right-hand corner of the FrontPage window. It's a good idea to keep this figure at less than 30 seconds. If you imagine doing nothing but waiting for over 30 seconds, you can understand how a site visitor might feel.

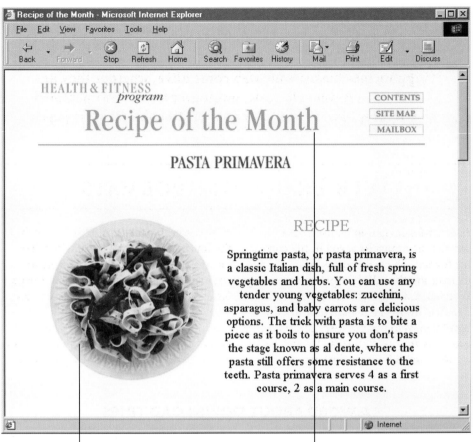

This is a JPEG image. It has been saved as a JPEG image because it is a photograph containing fine detail and many colors.

This is an example of a GIF image. It consists of high-quality type on a white background and is being used as a banner for the page.

JPEG OR GIF?

A basic rule of thumb is to use JPEG for photographs and GIF for almost everything else. The GIF image above consists of green lettering on a white background and is best saved as a GIF. But the pasta photograph is best saved as a JPEG. If in doubt, save the images in both formats and view them in a browser. Use the smaller file-size image if they appear the same.

INSERTING AN IMAGE

FrontPage's visual editing makes working with images very easy. But you need to acquire them from somewhere. A common way is to use a scanner to scan an image and save it on your PC. You can also save images directly from your browser when viewing other people's websites (although beware of copyright laws). Collections of images are available, usually on CD-ROM. And if you know how to create graphics, you can make your own images using graphics software.

1 SELECTING AN IMAGE

● Create a new page and save it as **pasta pages.htm**.
● Once you have an image saved as a GIF or JPEG, position the cursor at the place where you want the image to appear, and from the **Insert** menu choose **Picture** and then **From File**.
● The **Picture** dialog box appears. Using the **Look in:** box, navigate to the location of your image.
● If you highlight the image you will see a preview of it in the window at right.
● Click on **OK** to insert the image onto the page.

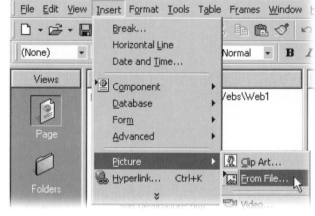

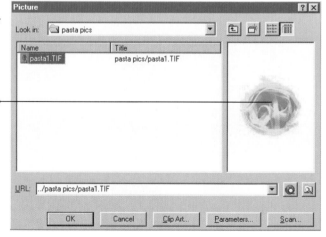

Image preview ●

pasta pages.htm

The trick with pasta is to bite a piece as it boils to ensu the stage known as al dente, where the pasta still offer: resistance to the teeth. Pasta primavera serves 4 as a f as a main course.

The web image as it appears in the FrontPage workspace window

2 SAVING THE IMAGE

● When you save the page, FrontPage displays the **Save Embedded Files** dialog box, which asks if you want to save the image you have just inserted. Click on **OK**, and a copy of the image file is saved into your web.

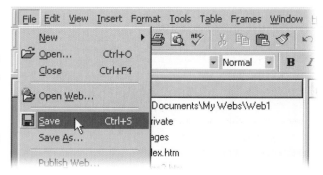

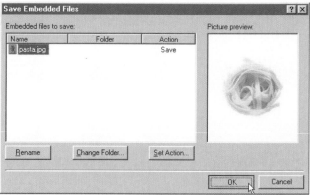

3 INSERTING CLIP ART

● FrontPage comes with a large selection of Clip Art for use in your website. Place the cursor where you want to position your clip art and from the Insert menu select **Picture** and then **Clip Art**.

● Scroll down the icons in the Clip Art Gallery and click on **Food & Dining**.

● There are two clips available. Click on the basket of bread and click on the **Insert clip** icon.

● The clip is oversized, so right-click on it, select **Picture Properties** from the menu, and click on the **Appearance** tab in the **Picture Properties** dialog box. Click in the **Specify size** check box and enter **169** in the **Width** box – the figure in the **Height** box changes automatically to retain the proportions. Click on **OK**. The **Preview** screen can be used to show how the clip appears in your web page.

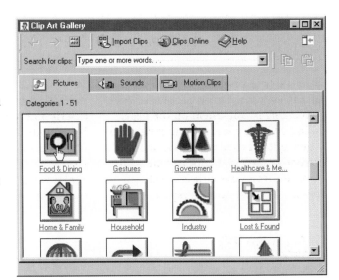

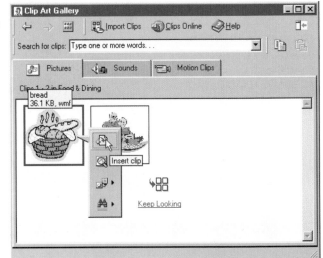

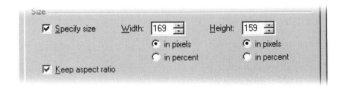

IMAGE PROPERTIES

Once you have placed an image on a page you can alter some of its properties, such as changing its alignment on the page, adding invisible space around the border, or giving it a textual name (known as **alternative text**) that appears when you move your mouse over it in a web browser. This last point is especially important as it can be an excellent aid to navigation, as well as being a useful description of what the image represents. It is also the text that will appear as the image downloads. This can be helpful to a visitor with a slow connection because it allows them to have some idea of what the image will be before it appears.

1 ALTERNATIVE TEXT

● First, open a page containing an image to which you want to apply alternative text (see above). Right-click on the image and choose **Picture Properties** from the pop-up menu that appears.

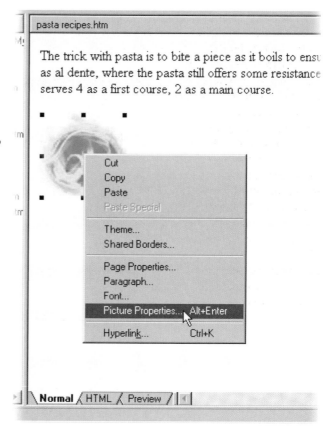

pasta recipes.htm

The trick with pasta is to bite a piece as it boils to ensu as al dente, where the pasta still offers some resistance serves 4 as a first course, 2 as a main course.

Cut
Copy
Paste
Paste Special
Theme...
Shared Borders...
Page Properties...
Paragraph...
Font...
Picture Properties...   Alt+Enter
Hyperlink...   Ctrl+K

Normal / HTML / Preview /

● The **Picture Properties** dialog box appears. In the section labeled **Alternative representations**, type **Pasta** into the **Text** box.

● When a visitor to your site waits for the page to download, **Pasta** will appear where the image is eventually positioned.

Low-res substitute
If you have a low-resolution image of the picture, you can enter its file name in the **Low-Res** box, and it will be displayed while the full image is downloading.

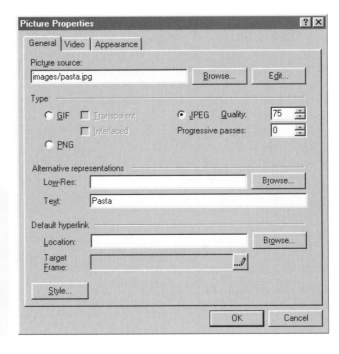

2 APPEARANCE OF THE IMAGE

● Now click on the **Appearance** tab in the **Picture Properties** dialog box. Perhaps you would like to make the image align to the right of the page. Click on the **Alignment** drop-down arrow and choose **Right** from the list.

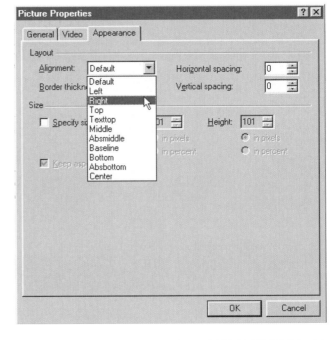

3 IMAGE SPACING

● You can put some invisible space around an image so that there is some space between it and any text that may be nearby.

● Again, in the **Appearance** tab in the **Picture Properties** dialog box, type **5** into both the **Horizontal spacing** and **Vertical spacing** boxes. The units are pixels. Click on **OK** to save the changes you have made.

● The image moves across to the right-hand side of the page surrounded by the invisible space.

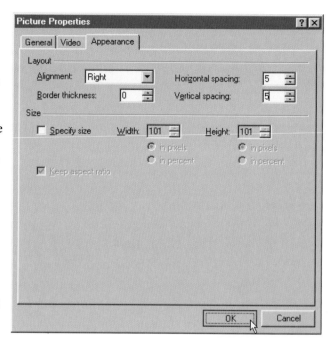

4 PREVIEWING THE IMAGE

● You can now see the results of your changes in the FrontPage workspace window. Try clicking the **Preview** tab and then moving your mouse over the image – the Alternative text appears.

Preview tab ●

CREATING LINKS

A compelling feature of the World Wide Web is that you can link pages to create a "web" of information. The link could be to a page in your site, or to a site on the other side of the world.

CREATING A LINK

Creating hyperlinks between web pages is one of the most fundamental skills you need when building a website. Without these links, a site would be nothing more than a collection of individual pages rather than a unified web of information. There are many types of link that you can make. You can link to another page in your site, or to someone else's site. You can create a link that sends an email, or you can place a link on an image. You can also make a link open in a new browser window. This section will show you how to master all these skills.

1 MAKING A TEXT LINK

● The simplest form of link is a text link. In this example we will make a link from the home page to the second page of the site.

● Open the home page, called **index.htm**, and type **Click here to go to the second page of my site.**

index.htm

Welcome to my home page!

This is some practice text that I'm typing in to see how Microsoft FrontPage 2000. Now I'm going to press t new paragraph.

Here's my third paragraph.

Click here to go to the second page of my site.

2 SELECTING TEXT TO LINK

● Now highlight the words **Click here** and choose **Hyperlink** from the foot of the **Insert** menu. The **Create Hyperlink** dialog box opens on screen.

● The pages in your website are listed. We want to link to the file called **page2.htm**, so click on that file. Its name appears in the URL box.

● Click on **OK** in order to create the link.

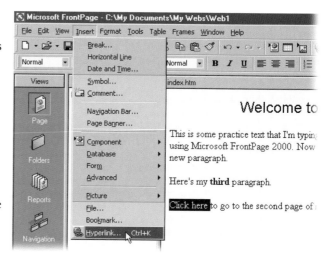

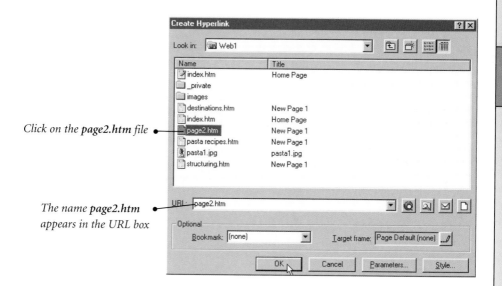

*Click on the **page2.htm** file*

*The name **page2.htm** appears in the URL box*

WHAT IS A URL?

URL means "Universal Resource Locator" – a web page address. Most start with **http://** (which tells the browser to use the HyperText Transfer Protocol – a communications protocol) followed by a web address beginning **www**. When you create a link, you are giving the browser a URL to link to.

3 TESTING THE LINK

● You will notice that the words **Click here** now change color and have a line underneath them. This shows that they are linked to another page. Change to **Preview** mode and try clicking on the link. It will take you to the file called **page2.htm**.

index.htm

Welcome to my hon

This is some practice text that I'm typing in to see how using Microsoft FrontPage 2000. Now I'm going to p new paragraph.

Here's my **third** paragraph.

Click here to go to the second page of my site.

index.htm

Welcome to my homepage!

This is some practice text that I'm typing in to see how Microsoft FrontPage 2000. Now I'm going to press th new paragraph.

Here's my third paragraph.

Click here to go to the second page of my site.

Normal / HTML / **Preview** /

Saving before linking

It is important to save your web page before creating any links in it. If links are created before the web page is saved, the links will not be updated if you change the location of your page.

4 CREATING AN EXTERNAL LINK

● Now let's make a link to another website. On the home page type **I made this site using FrontPage from Microsoft**.

● Now highlight the word **Microsoft** and click on **Insert** in the menu bar and choose **Hyperlink**.

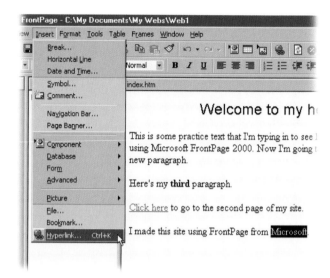

● This time, rather than choosing another page in your site, type: **http:// www.microsoft.com** in the URL box and click on **OK**.

● This creates a link to the Microsoft website. You can make links to other sites in the same way by typing in different URLs.

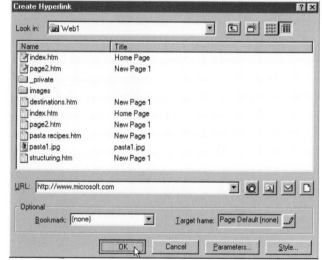

5 EMAIL LINKS

● Another useful link to make is an email link. When a visitor clicks on such a link, their email program launches and they can send an email to the address specified on your page. To make this kind of link, highlight some text as before and choose **Hyperlink** from the **Insert** menu again.

● This time, click on the button with the image of an envelope on it. You'll see the **Create E-mail Hyperlink** box appear. Here you should type in the email address to which you want to create a link. Then click on **OK**.

● The URL in the **Create Hyperlink** window changes and now begins with **mailto:** indicating an email link. Click on **OK** to create the new link.

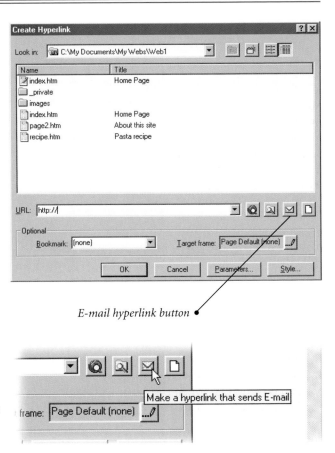

E-mail hyperlink button ●

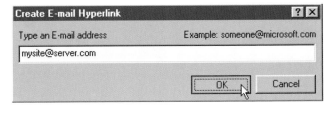

Recipient's email address ●

6 A LINK IN A NEW WINDOW

● Sometimes it can be useful to open a link in a new browser window. For example, you might want to send a visitor to another website, but also want to keep your own site open on their desktop. To do this, select some text or an image as before, but this time click on the pencil icon to the right of the **Target frame** in the **Create Hyperlink** dialog box.

● In the **Target Frame** dialog box, choose **New Window** from the **Common targets** list, and then click on **OK**.

● Now enter the URL of another website in the URL box and click on **OK**. When a visitor clicks on the link you have created, it will open in a new window in their browser.

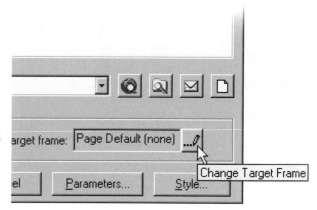

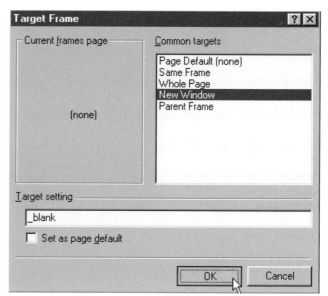

New page – new link
Clicking the **New Page** button to the right of the E-mail hyperlink button allows you to create a new page in your web and to create a hyperlink to it.

USING TABLES

The use of tables in your website is a great way to present information in a clear and organized style. Tables can also be used to create more complex page layouts.

CREATING A TABLE

Creating tables in FrontPage is a very straightforward process. The most common use of tables is for laying out information in a style that is easy to read and understand. Let's take the example of an online business that sells guitars. They want to have a page on their website showing their current inventory, so that customers can quickly see what is available over their online system. This type of information is best presented in a table. As you will see, FrontPage gives you a great deal of control over how your table appears on your web page.

1 INSERTING A TABLE

● First create a new page in your web and call it **inventory.htm**. At the top of the page type **Our Current Inventory** and press [Enter←].
● Click on **Table** in the menu bar, choose **Insert** and then **Table**. The **Insert Table** dialog box appears.

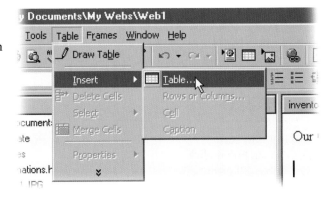

ROWS, COLUMNS, AND CELLS

Every table consists of table cells. Cells are the rectangular boxes in your table. A row is a horizontal series of table cells, and a column is a vertical series.

2 TABLE OPTIONS

● You can tell FrontPage how many rows and columns you want in your table. To create a table with 6 rows and 3 columns (you can add more later), enter these values into the **Rows** and **Columns** boxes.

● The **Layout** section contains options for greater control over how your table will look. First, specify the width by entering **400** and selecting **In pixels** – this means the table is 400 pixels wide (a pixel is a unit of measurement for computer displays).

● We want a border on the table. Enter **1** in the **Border size** box. Then click on **OK**.

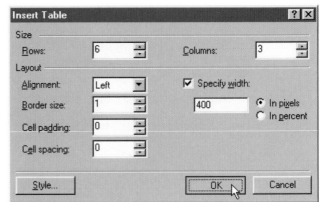

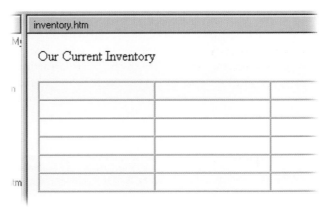

3 ENTERING DATA

● You can now start entering data. Either click in each table cell or press the Tab key to move to the next cell. The cell width alters according to the length of text that is entered. Fill in the table as shown in this example.

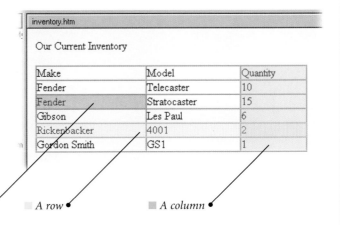

■ *A table cell* ●   ■ *A row* ●   ■ *A column* ●

4 BACKGROUND COLOR

● One way to make a table stand out more is to use background colors. Highlight the first row of the table by dragging across it with the mouse.

● Now right-click on the row and then in the pop-up menu that appears, click on **Cell Properties**. The **Cell Properties** dialog box opens.

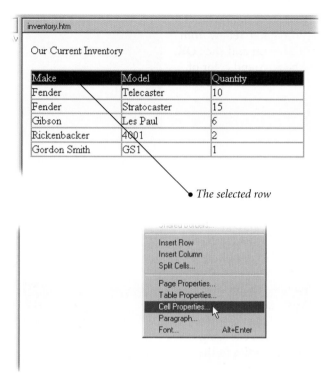

The selected row

Flowing text

If you want text to flow around a table that does not fill the width of the page, click on **Table** in the menu bar and select **Properties** and then **Table**. Click on the arrow next to **Float**, select **Left** or **Right** from the pull-down and click on **OK**. The table will move in that direction to make space for text, which will flow around it starting from the second row.

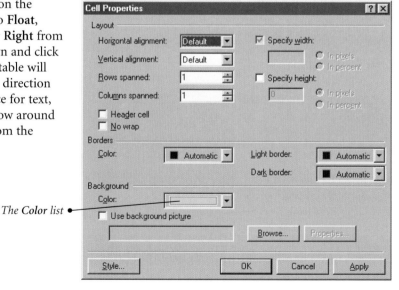

The Color list

● Under the **Background** section, select **Yellow** from the **Color** list and click **OK**. The background color of the row changes to yellow.

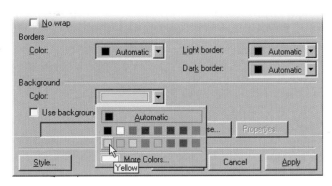

5 CELL PADDING AND SPACING

● The table is looking better, but the text is still quite close to the table's border lines. Change this by right-clicking anywhere in the table and choosing **Table Properties** in the pop-up menu.

● Enter a value of **2** in both the **Cell padding** and **Cell spacing** boxes. This inserts some extra space between the table entries, making them easier to read.

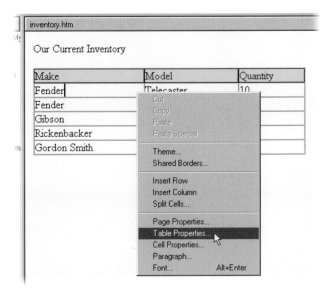

The Cell padding and Cell spacing boxes ●

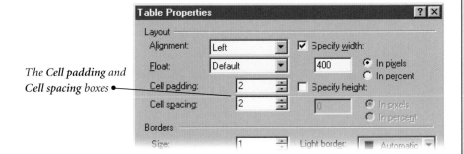

6 ALIGNING DATA

● Each cell in the table is aligned to the left by default. However, perhaps you would like to align the **Quantity** column to the center. Highlight the entire column by dragging with the mouse from the top to the bottom of the column.

● Now click on the **Center** button on the Formatting toolbar 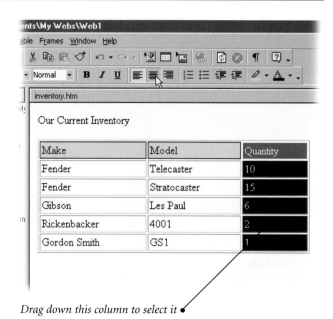 to change the alignment to the center.

Drag down this column to select it ●

7 ADDING A NEW ROW

● The table would look better with a new row at the top containing a title. Position the cursor in the first cell of the table and right-click. Then choose **Insert Row** from the pop-up menu.

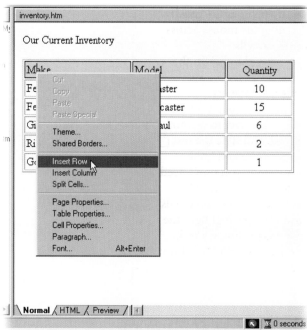

• This inserts a new blank row of three cells above the top row of the table.

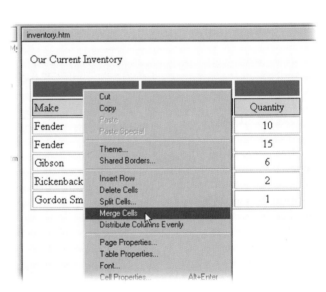

8 MERGING TABLE CELLS

• Perhaps the new first row would look best as one long table cell. To merge the three cells together, highlight the entire row by dragging the mouse across the three cells.

• Next, right-click in the row and choose **Merge Cells** from the list.

• The three cells are now one. Type **Inventory** into the cell, and style the text as font **Arial** and **bold**.

• Although you don't need to do it now, it's easy to split the cell into three cells again. Simply highlight the long cell, right-click in it, and choose **Split Cells** from the pop-up menu.

USING TABLES FOR PAGE LAYOUT

Using tables with invisible borders around cells means that images and text can be placed with great accuracy. In the next example, a list of ingredients for a recipe has been created, but the same layout methods can be applied to your own images. First, create a new page in your web and save it as **ingredients_table.htm**.

1 CREATE A NEW TABLE

● Place the cursor at the top of the new page and from the **Table** menu choose **Insert** and then **Table**.

● In the **Insert Table** dialog box, create a table with 4 rows and 5 columns. Specify the width as **500** pixels and make sure that the **Border size** is set at **0**.

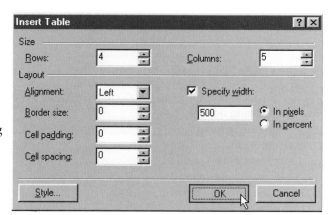

2 CHANGE THE COLUMN WIDTHS

● Although the border lines are invisible when viewed in a web browser, FrontPage displays them as thin lines as a design aid.

● Select the first column by dragging down it with the mouse so it is highlighted, and then right-click and choose **Cell Properties** from the pop-up menu.

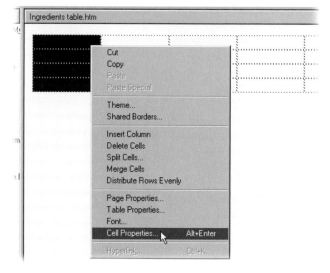

● In the **Cell Properties** dialog box click in the **Specify width** check box, then specify a width of **5 percent**.

● Repeat this process for the third and fifth columns to produce the ingredients table as shown.

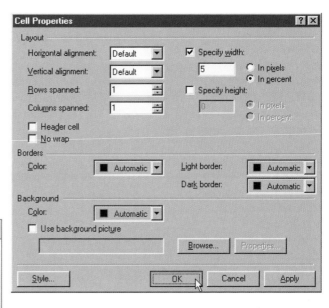

EXPERIMENTATION

This is just one example of a table being used as a grid for laying out a page. There are countless variations, and the best way to learn is by experimentation. Try creating other layouts with different column widths and other combinations of rows and columns.

3 MERGE THE FIRST ROW

● Merge the first row of the table by highlighting it, right-clicking in it, and choosing **Merge Cells**.

● Next, type in a title for the page, highlight it, center it, and set it to font size **6**.

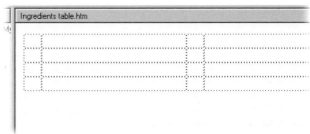

4 INSERT IMAGES

● Now put some images into some of the blank cells on the table. This is the same process as inserting an image on a page. Click in a cell and from the **Insert** menu choose **Picture** and then **From File**. Navigate to the image you require and click on **OK**.

● In the example, three images have been inserted into the cells that make up the second column.

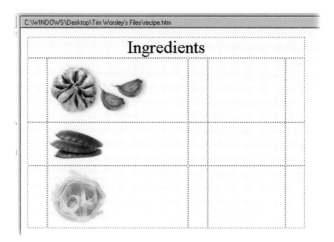

5 ADD TEXT

● You can now type in some text to accompany the images. Type the text into the empty cells in the fourth column as you can see here.

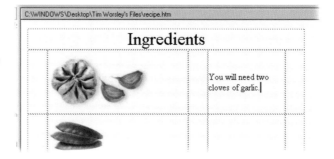

ALTERNATIVE TABLES

You can also insert tables by clicking the **Tables** icon in the Standard toolbar and dragging the cursor across the grid to select cells and columns. This method can also be used to insert a table within a table, for more complex layouts of images and text.

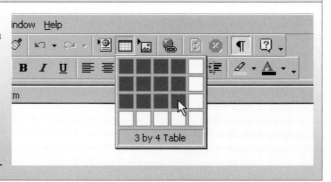

6 PREVIEW THE PAGE

● Click on the **Preview** tab to see how the page will look in the browser. Notice how the table border lines are no longer visible. The table structure we have created means that each element on the page is correctly positioned.

Preview tab •

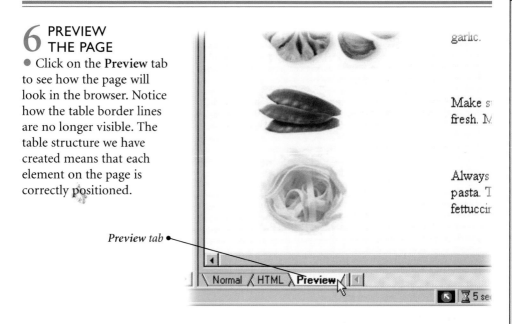

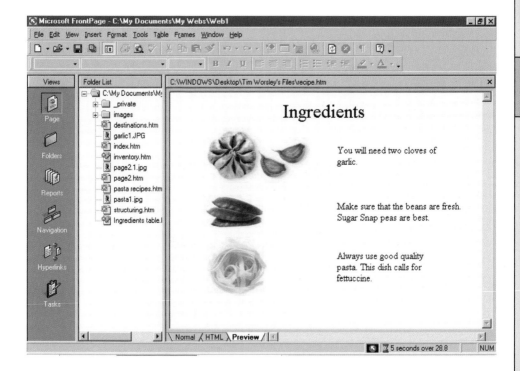

USING FORMS

Forms add an extra dimension to your website by letting your visitors send information back to you. This makes your website much more interactive, and potentially much more useful.

FORM ELEMENTS

A form consists of a series of labeled "fields" into which visitors can provide feedback. The form can then be submitted in various ways. For example, the information can be saved in a text file and analyzed later using a spreadsheet program. FrontPage makes creating forms very easy, allowing you to concentrate on the content of the form rather than on the computer code that allows the form to work. In these next pages you will see how to create a simple visitor-feedback form.

1 INSERTING A FORM

● Create a new page ☐ in your web and name it **feedback.htm**. Then type in some introductory text similar to the example shown here.

● Next, position the cursor beneath the text and from the **Insert** menu choose **Form** and then **Form**.

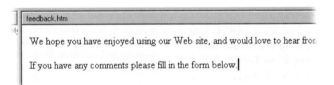

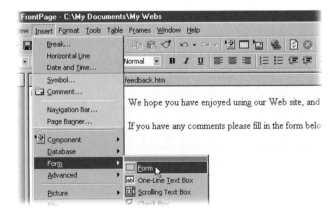

● A blank form is inserted, which contains a **Submit** button and a **Reset** button.

> feedback.htm
>
> We hope you have enjoyed using our Web site, and would love to hear from y
>
> If you have any comments please fill in the form below.
>
> [Submit] [Reset]

2 CREATE A FIELD LABEL

● Press [Enter ↵] twice to give you room above the buttons (note that the area of the form is marked by a dotted frame). At the top of the form, type **Name:** as a field label, followed by the [Tab] key to give some space.

> feedback.htm
>
> We hope you have enjoyed using our Web site, and would love to hear from y
>
> If you have any comments please fill in the form below.
>
> Name:
>
> [Submit] [Reset]

3 ADD A TEXT BOX

● From the **Insert** menu choose **Form** and then **One-Line Text Box**. A rectangular area appears, which is where your visitor can type their name. Press [Enter ↵] to start a new line.

● Repeat the previous step so you have fields for **Email**, **Telephone**, and **Fax**.

● Use the [Tab ⇆] key to align each of the text boxes.

> Microsoft FrontPage - C:\My Documents\My Webs
>
> File Edit View Insert Format Tools Table Frames Window Help
>
> Break...
> Horizontal Line
> Date and Time...
> Symbol...
> Comment...
> Navigation Bar...
> Page Banner...
> Component
> Database
> Form   ▶ Form
> Advanced   One-Line Text Box
> Picture   Scrolling Text Box
>   Check Box
>
> feedback.htm
>
> We hope you have enjoyed using our W
>
> If you have any comments please fill in th
>
> Name:

> Name: [   ]
>
> [Submit] [Reset]

4 A SCROLLING TEXT BOX

● Next you can insert an area where a visitor can write some comments. This is a different type of form field called a **Scrolling Text Box**.

● Type **Comments:** as a field label, press [Enter←], and from the **Insert** menu choose **Form** and then **Scrolling Text Box**.

● You'll see a larger text box with scrollbars appear on the page.

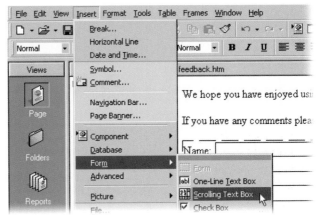

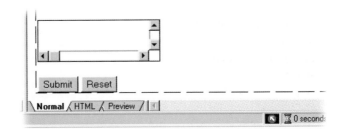

5 INSERTING RADIO BUTTONS

● Below the Comments box, type **Would you like to be added to our e-mail list?**. You can now add two radio buttons to give your visitor a choice of **Yes** or **No**. From the **Insert** menu choose **Form** and then **Radio Button** to insert the button.

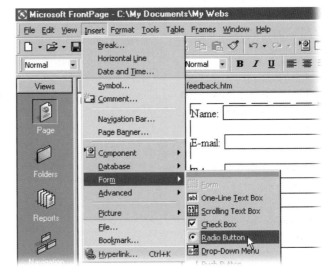

● Then type **Yes**. Press the
[Tab] key, insert another
radio button, and type **No**.

6 CHANGING A FIELD'S VALUE

● When the form is
submitted, it will record
which radio button the
visitor clicked, but you need
to give the button a
meaningful name or "value."

● Double-click on the first
radio button to access the
Radio Button Properties
dialog box.

● Type **OnList** in the
Group Name box, and **Yes**
in the **Value** box, followed
by **OK**. Repeat the process
for the **No** radio button. Still
type **OnList** in the **Group
Name** box, but this time
type **No** in the **Value** box.

● Now, when the form is
submitted, it records either
"Yes" or "No" for the **OnList**
field, making the results
easier to read.

7 USING DROP-DOWN MENUS

● Under the radio buttons,
type **Where did you hear
about us?**, choose **Form**
from the **Insert** menu, and
then **Drop-Down Menu**.

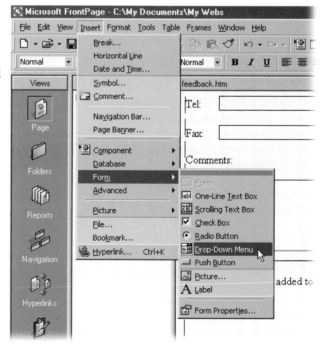

● You'll see an arrow next to a small box, which is the drop-down menu.

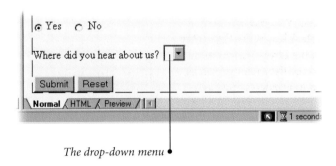

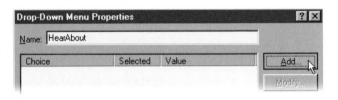

The drop-down menu ●

8 ADDING TO THE MENU

● You need to add items to the Drop-Down Menu. Double-click on it to open the **Drop-Down Menu Properties** dialog box.

● First, type **HearAbout** in the **Name** box (to name the menu), and then click on the **Add** button to see the **Add Choice** dialog box. This is where you can add items to the menu. Type in **Television** into the **Choice** box. Then click on **Selected** in the **Initial State** area. This will make **Television** the default choice when the visitor first sees the menu.

● Click **OK**, and then click on the **Add** button again to repeat the process to add **Radio**, **Newspaper**, and **Other** to the **Choice** list. For these choices, choose **Not Selected** in the **Initial State** area – only one choice can be initially selected – in this case, **Television**.

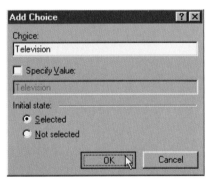

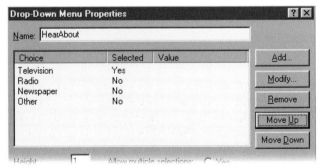

- Click on **OK** and save the page. You should now see **Television** as the first entry in the **Drop-Down Menu**. To see the menu properly, go to **Preview** mode and click on the arrow next to **Television**.

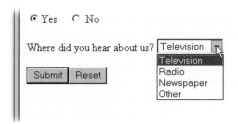

9 STORING A FORM'S RESULTS

- You now have all the fields we require on the form – the final step is to tell FrontPage how to store the data when a visitor submits the form.

- Right-click anywhere on the form and choose **Form Properties** in the pop-up menu that appears.

- By default, FrontPage stores the results of the form in a text file called **form_results.txt** in the **_private** folder of your website (this is a special folder that can only be seen by you). Click on **OK** to accept this default.

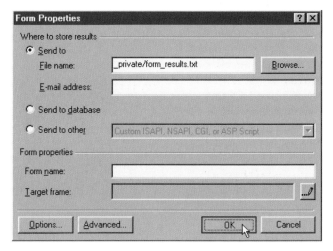

VIEWING THE RESULTS OF A FORM

To view the results of a form, open the **_private** folder and double-click on **form_results.txt**. The file opens in a text editor and you will see each entry as one line of text with each field separated by a comma. This type of text file is a CSV (Comma Separated Values) file, and can easily be imported into most database or spreadsheet programs, such as Microsoft Access or Excel.

FRONTPAGE COMPONENTS

In addition to creating forms from scratch, FrontPage comes with a selection of prebuilt forms and other functions that you can easily use in your website. They require the FrontPage Server Extensions in order to work correctly, and are very simple to use. The two most popular components are the hit counter and the search form. The hit counter is a numerical display that records the number of times that a page has been requested by people browsing the web, and the search form allows the visitors to your site to search it by using a keyword.

1 INSERTING A HIT COUNTER

● Open the home page of your site, and at the bottom of the page type **This page has been requested**, followed by a space. Now choose **Component** from the **Insert** menu, followed by **Hit Counter**. You'll see the **Hit Counter Properties** dialog box appear on the screen.

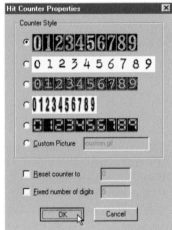

FrontPage server extensions

2 CHOOSE A STYLE

● You can choose a variety of graphical styles for the counter. You can also choose to reset the counter to a specific figure, and to limit the counter to a fixed number of digits. After you have made your selections, click on **OK**.

● When you look at your page, you'll see that FrontPage just displays a placeholder for the hit counter – this is because

I made this site using FrontPage from Microsoft.

Please e-mail me your comments.

This page has been requested [**Hit Counter**] times.

the counter will only function after you have published the page to a web server.

● Finish off the hit counter by adding a space after the placeholder and then

typing **times**. When the hit counter eventually becomes operational, it will now display a sentence that contains the total number of instances when the page has been requested.

3 USING A SEARCH PAGE

● You may have used search facilities that have been provided on pages in other websites. Here's how to create your own.

● Create a new page in your web and name it **search.htm**. This will be the page containing the search component. Add some introductory text at the top of the page – for example, **You can search our site by typing in a keyword into the Search box below:**.

● Now choose **Component** from the **Insert** menu, followed by **Search Form**. The **Search Form Properties** dialog box will now open.

● You can customize the appearance of the search form by amending the values in this window. For example, to make the search box longer, type **30** into the **Width in characters** box.

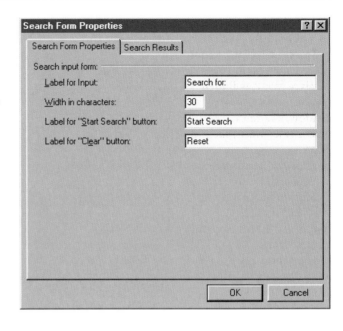

SEARCH RESULTS OPTIONS

● Next, click on the **Search Results** tab of the **Search Form Properties** dialog box. This is where you tell FrontPage how to display the results of the search. For example, for the most comprehensive results, tick the three check boxes under **Display options**.

● When a visitor sees the results of their search, they see the file name, file size, file creation date, and a score (the higher the score the closer the match). Click OK to save your changes.

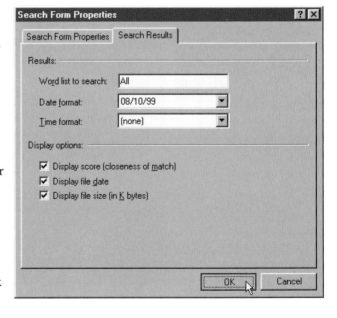

5 THE SEARCH FORM AT WORK

● The search form cannot work until it is published to a web server. It will then appear in the browser window, and the visitor can type in a keyword, such as **pasta**.

● After clicking on the **Start Search** button, the browser window refreshes itself and presents a list of results in a table below the search form.

● The visitor can then click on a document title to jump to that page.

The results of the search are displayed here ●

PUBLISHING THE SITE

Once you have created a website you can check it for errors, and then make it accessible to others by using FrontPage to publish it onto the internet.

CHECKING FOR BROKEN LINKS

One of the most frustrating experiences when browsing a website is to click on a hyperlink, only to find that the target page cannot be found. This is normally due to a broken link, which may have been typed incorrectly, or the page may have been renamed, moved, or deleted. FrontPage has built-in features to deal with the most common causes of links being broken, but there are times when broken links will still occur. FrontPage has a detailed **Reports** view that identifies broken links (in addition to other summaries) and has features to help you fix them. Begin by opening a page that contains links to other pages. In this case, the file, **index.htm**.

1 **SWITCH TO REPORTS VIEW**
● Click on **View** in the menu bar, select **Reports** and then **Site Summary**. The **Site Summary** page opens containing detailed information about your site.

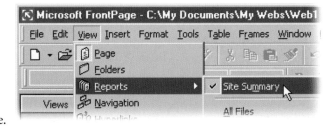

Broken Hyperlinks			
Status	Hyperlink	In Page	Page Title
⚭ Broken	page_two.htm	index.htm	Home Page
? Unknown	http://www.microsoft.com	index.htm	Home Page

2 FIND BROKEN LINKS

● Double-clicking on the **Broken** hyperlink line displays a detailed list. Earlier, a link was created to **page2.htm** 🔲. Now we have deliberately created a broken link by renaming the link as **page_two.htm**.

● The first line of the list shows the broken link on the home page. Double-click on that line.

● In the **Edit Hyperlink** dialog box, type the correct name of the page in the **Replace hyperlink with** box. Click on **Replace**.

● The hyperlink is amended and you are returned to the **Broken Hyperlinks** report page. The corrected link is no longer listed.

● After working through other broken links in your site, the **Broken Hyperlinks count** on the **Site Summary** page should read **0**.

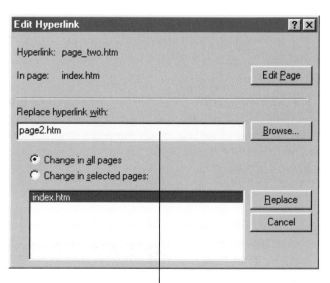

Type the correct link in this box ●

OTHER INFORMATION IN REPORTS VIEW

You will have noticed that there is a lot of other interesting information on the **Site Summary** report page, such as how many pages in your site would be slow to load, or how many pages have been recently added to the site. For most of the lines in the report, you can double-click on the line that interests you and see a more detailed report for that topic. Why not experiment and take a look at some of these other reports? They can be very helpful in analyzing your website.

Selecting text to link

PUBLISHING TO A WEB SERVER

When you are satisfied that your site contains no further errors, it's time to publish it to the internet (sometimes called making the site "live"). However, before you do this, you must have somewhere to publish it to – in other words, you need access to a web server. A web server is typically a powerful computer with a high bandwidth connection to the internet. It runs special software that handles requests for pages, runs scripts, and "serves up" web pages. You may have access to a web server via your company, in which case you can contact your technical support staff and obtain the details you'll need for publishing. Alternatively, you can purchase space on a commercial web server.

1 FINDING A WEB SERVER

● Before you start, make sure you have all the necessary details about your web server. You will need the URL of the server, and possibly a name as well as a password in order to gain access to the server.

● Make sure your computer is connected to the internet and choose **Publish Web** from the **File** menu. Type the URL of your web server in the box provided in the **Publish Web** dialog box. We have used an imaginary

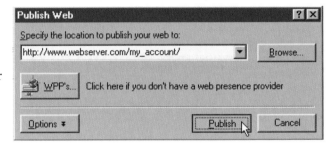

name in this example. If you haven't already found a web server on which to publish your site, you can click on the **WPP's** button. Doing so will take you to an area on Microsoft's website where you can find a

suitable provider of web server space (in FrontPage terminology, these are called Web Presence Providers). You can then sign up with one of these Providers and continue with the publishing of your site.

FRONTPAGE SERVER EXTENSIONS

The web server you use should support the Front-Page Server Extensions. These Extensions allow you to use features such as the Hit Counter and the Search Form. They also allow the site to be admin-istered remotely and to be password protected. You can still publish your site without the Extensions, but you will not be able to take advantage of the features mentioned.

2 THE PUBLISHING PROCESS

● When you are ready, click **Publish** in order to start the publishing process. FrontPage will then attempt to connect to your targeted web server.

● If you are asked for a name and password, enter these details when prompted. FrontPage will then start transferring (or "uploading") the files that make up your website. This may take a few minutes, depending on the size of

your site and the speed of your internet connection. You will see a progress indicator showing how the publishing process is going.

● When all the files have been published you'll see

the window that is shown in the screen shot above.

● You can click on the **Click here to view your published web site** hyperlink to view your site in your web browser.

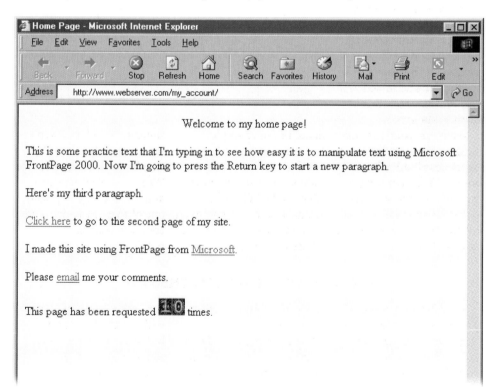

TESTING THE SITE IN A BROWSER

Congratulations! Your website should now be "live" on the internet and available for visitors to browse. But before they do, it's a good idea to check the site yourself using a web browser and make sure that everything is working as it should. Clearly the most important thing is to check that all the pages have been published successfully. You can do this by visiting each page in your site and checking that it loads into your browser window correctly. In doing so, you are also checking that each link is pointing to the right place. You can also check any forms or FrontPage components you have used, such as the Hit Counter or the Search Form.

1 ACCESSING YOUR SITE

● To check your website, connect to the internet, launch a web browser and type the address of the site into the **Address** box.

● Next, test the hyperlinks in your site by clicking on each link and making sure the target page loads correctly. In this example, click on **Click here** in the fourth paragraph and ensure that **page2.htm** appears on screen.

● Test any other links you have made in the same way.

If the link is working correctly,
Page 2 *should appear* ●

2 TEST THE HIT COUNTER

● Make sure the Hit Counter is working correctly by loading the home page and checking the Hit Counter paragraph. Click on **Refresh** in your browser window – the Counter display should increase by one digit.

This page has been requested **14** times.

This page has been requested **15** times.

3 TEST THE COMMENTS FORM

● Try filling out the Comments form you created earlier with some test information, such as your own name and details.

● Now click on the **Submit** button and make sure you see the FrontPage response screen with a review of the form's information.

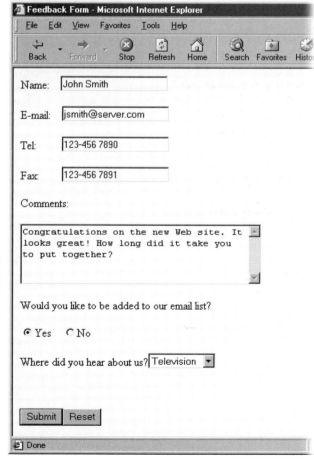

Spread the word...
After you have checked the site thoroughly give yourself a pat on the back – your site is now up and running! Remember to give out the URL of your site to friends and business contacts so they can see your work.

GLOSSARY

ADDRESS BOOK
A central store of contact information for retrieving easily and simply.

ATTACHMENT
Almost any type of file can be sent with an email by attaching it to a message that you send.

BOOLEAN MODIFIERS
Words (AND, OR, NOT) that help you to modify the terms of a keyword search.

BROWSER
See Web browser.

CHANNEL
A website designed to deliver internet content to your computer. If you are running an active desktop in Windows 98, you can access channel websites directly from the desktop without using Internet Explorer.

COMPRESSION
A system to reduce the disk space taken up by a computer file, often to make the image faster to download.

DIAL-UP NETWORKING SOFTWARE
Windows 98 software that enables you to connect to the internet via a service provider.

DIRECTORY SERVICE
A powerful search tool designed to help you find people and businesses worldwide.

DOWNLOAD
The process of transferring a file from a remote computer to your computer.

EMAIL (ELECTRONIC MAIL)
A system for sending messages between computers that are linked over a network.

FAVORITES
A website for which you have created an electronic "bookmark" enabling you to access it from the Favorite menu in the toolbar.

FREEWARE
Software that can be freely used and distributed, but the author retains copyright.

GIF (GRAPHICS INTERCHANGE FORMAT)
A widely used file format for web-based images.

HOME PAGE
The first page you see at a website, typically containing a welcome message and hyperlinks to other pages.

HTML (HYPERTEXT MARKUP LANGUAGE)
A computer language used to create web pages. HTML consists of tags that describe how a page should be displayed.

HYPERLINKS
A "hot" part of a web page (e.g., text, image, table etc.) that links to another part of the same document or another document on the internet.

HYPERTEXT
Text that contains links to other parts of a document, or to documents held on another computer.

INBOX
This is the name of the folder in which Outlook Express stores incoming messages by default.

INTERNET
The network of interconnected computers that communicate using the TCP/IP protocol.

INTERNET SERVICE PROVIDER (ISP)
A commercial organization that provides access to the internet.

JPEG (JOINT PHOTO-GRAPHIC EXPERTS GROUP)
A file format for web-based images, particularly for photographic images.

MAIL SERVER
A large computer used by ISPs to store email messages and relay them over the internet.

MAILBOX
The area on a mail server used to store email messages for a particular email address.

METASEARCH PROGRAM
A program that enables you to query simultaneously the databases of a number of search providers.

MODEM (MODULATOR-DEMODULATOR)
An electronic device that allows computers to communicate via a telephone line by converting signals to and from analog and binary forms.

NETIQUETTE
An unwritten code of conduct for the proper and polite usage of the internet.

NETWORK
A group of interconnected computers that exchange data.

NEWS SERVER
A large computer used to relay newsgroup messages over the newsgroup network, Usenet.

NEWSGROUPS
Internet discussion groups on specific topics, where people can post information, exchange comments, or contribute to public debates.

NEWSREADER
Software that enables you to access and use newsgroups. Outlook Express has newsreader capabilities.

OFFLINE
Not connected to the internet.

ONLINE
Connected to the internet.

OUTBOX
The folder in which Outlook Express stores sent messages.

PATH
The address of a file on a computer system.

PIXEL
A unit of measurement for computer displays. A display consists of a series of pixels that display images on the screen.

PLUG-IN
A program that adds features to a web browser so that it can handle files containing, for example, 3-D and multimedia elements.

PROTOCOL
A set of rules that two computers are required to follow when they communicate.

PUBLISH
You publish a website by sending its pages to a server.

SCANNER
A device that creates digital versions of images by scanning them with a beam of light.

SEARCH DIRECTORY
Large database of website URLs and site descriptions organized by category and, in some cases, accompanied by editors' reviews.

SEARCH ENGINE
Software that searches for information on the internet based on your search criteria.

SEARCH PROVIDER
Any organization that provides search services for internet users.

SERVER
A computer that allows users to connect to it and share data and resources held on it.

SERVICE PROVIDER
See Internet Service Provider.

SHAREWARE
Software that is made freely available for use on a try-before-you-buy basis.

SPIDER
A program developed by search providers to trawl the web to collect information. Spiders can also be referred to as crawlers, worms, and web robots (or *bots*).

TCP/IP (TRANSMISSION CONTROL PROTOCOL/ INTERNET PROTOCOL
The two essential internet protocols that define how data must be transferred between two computers across a network.

URL (UNIVERSAL RESOURCE LOCATOR)
An address on the internet. You type a URL into your browser to visit a website.

USENET
A network of computer systems that carry the internet discussion groups called newsgroups.

V-STANDARDS
Worldwide electronic telecommunications standards that govern programming commands and data compression standards used by modems and other devices.

WEB BROWSER
A program used for viewing and accessing information and sites on the web. Microsoft Internet Explorer and Netscape Navigator are the two most widely used and popular web browsers.

WEB PAGE
A single page on a website that can contain text, images, sound, video, and other elements.

WEB SERVER
A computer with a high-speed connection to the internet that "serves up" web pages.

WEBSITE
A collection of web pages that are linked together in a "web."

WIZARD
A series of prompts to accomplish a specific task.

WORLD WIDE WEB (WWW, W3, THE WEB)
All the websites on the internet that are linked together to form a global "web" of information.

INDEX

ACKNOWLEDGMENTS

PUBLISHER'S ACKNOWLEDGMENTS
Dorling Kindersley would like to thank the following:

Indexing Specialists, Hove.

Paul Mattock of APM, Brighton, for commissioned photography.

Microsoft Corporation for permission to reproduce screens
from within Microsoft® FrontPage®, Microsoft® Internet Explorer,
and Microsoft® Outlook® Express.

1stdirect.comaltavista.com; askjeeves.com; bbc.co.uk;
benjerry.com; bigfoot.com; club-europe.co.uk; cnn.com;
deja.com; demon.net; directhit.com; dmoz.org; dogpile.com; eidos.co.uk;
excite.com; freebeeb.net; gamesdomain.com; google.com; greenpeace.org;
hotbot.lycos.com; infoseek.com; ksc.nasa.gov; looksmart.com;
lycos.com (© 2000 Lycos, Inc.); metacrawler.com; msn.com; mus.com;
nasa.gov; netscape.com; nfl.com; northernlight.com; shop.com; unicef.org;
whitehouse.gov; winfiles.com; wnba.com; yahoo!; yellowpages.com

*Every effort has been made to trace the copyright holders.
The publisher apologizes for any unintentional omissions and would be pleased,
in such cases, to place an acknowledgment in future editions of this book.*

PICTURE CREDITS
The Stock Market/Jeff Zaruba (p.13)